POWER OVER TIME

POWER OVER TIME
Student Success with Time Management

JOAN FLEET / DENISE REAUME

HARCOURT
BRACE
CANADA

Harcourt Brace & Company, Canada

Toronto   Montreal   Orlando   Fort Worth   San Diego
Philadelphia   London   Sydney   Tokyo

Requests for permission to make copies of any part of the work should be mailed to: Permissions, College Division, Harcourt Brace & Company, Canada Inc., 55 Horner Avenue, Toronto, Ontario M8Z 4X6.

Every reasonable effort has been made to acquire permission for copyright material used in this text, and to acknowledge all such indebtedness accurately. Any errors and omissions called to the publisher's attention will be corrected in future printings.

Canadian Cataloguing in Publication Data
Fleet, Joan, 1939-
        Power over time: student success with time management

ISBN: 0-7747-3261-X

1. College students - Time management.   I. Reaume,
Denise.   II. Title.

LB3607.8.F54   1993   378.1'7'02812   C93-095182-4

Publisher: Heather McWhinney
Editor and Marketing Manager: Michael J. Young
Developmental Editor: Mario D'Alessandro
Director of Publishing Services: Jean Davies
Editorial Manager: Marcel Chiera
Production Manager: Sue-Ann Becker
Cover and Interior Design: Dave Peters, Brett Miller
Cover Illustration: Susan Dobson
Interior Illustrations: Tim Stover
Printing and Binding: Data Reproductions Corporation

This book was printed on acid-free paper.
1 2 3 4 5   97 96 95 94

OTHER TITLES AVAILABLE IN THE HARBRACE GUIDES TO STUDENT SUCCESS SERIES

Career Success: The Canadian Guide
Shannon Whelan

Fit to Print: The Canadian Student's Guide to Essay Writing, 2/e
Joanne Buckley

Learning for Success: Skills and Strategies for Canadian Students, 2/e
Joan Fleet, Fiona Goodchild, Richard Zajchowski

Making Your Mark: Learning to Do Well on Exams
Catherine Taylor
Second Edition revised and expanded by Heather Avery and Lucille Strath
Academic Skills Centre, Trent University

Transitions: It's Your Education
Greta Hofmann Nemiroff

Speaking for Success: The Canadian Guide
Anthony Lieb

"*Career Success* is a practical, positive, and useful guide for anyone who is seeking a fulfilling career. High school students, college students, and adults looking for a career change will all benefit from the practical advice and encouragement that the author gives."
Lindsey Holmes
Student
University of Calgary

"I couldn't have made a better choice than to buy *Fit to Print*. It was and is a life saver! Since that day I haven't received a mark below 80% on my essays."
Joanne R.
Student
Harbord Collegiate Institute

"*Fit to Print* takes a clear, concise, no-nonsense approach to the priblems of essay writing. Students (especially first-year students) will be able to understand this compact text and will not have to wade through it--as is the case with so many discursive composition books."
William Benzie
Professor
University of Victoria

"For its emphasis on well-written prose and its easy-to-follow, practical approach, *Fit to Print* is an invaluable aid for student writers in any discipline. Few books offer so much practical information to change student writing from a struggle to a success."
Jim McDonald and Karen Jacob
Instructors
Humber College

"*Learning for Success* is the book I used most during my first three weeks at school. Returning to school after twelve years, I found this to be the most helpful of all my textbooks in real practical terms. I would highly recommend this book for anyone just entering college or returning to school after having been away from the classroom for some time."
David Beattie
Student
Sir Sandford Fleming College

"For students who want to improve their study skills *Learning for Success* is an excellent resource. It explains the theory of study skills in understandable language, gives examples, and asks for student response."
Carol Potter
Instructor
Dawson College

"We offer a series of seminars, called Learning for Success, after this book. It is lucid, concise, orderly, and comprehensive, and serves a valuable purpose."
David Nimmo
Director of Student Services
University of Toronto

"*Learning for Success* is an excellent, practical guide for students in college and university, as well as senior high school level. It is a great resource for beginning counsellors, as it provides valuable information on various topics related to student success."
Irmo Marini
Counselling Co-ordinator
Lakehead University

"*Making Your Mark* reflects a lot of current experience working with students. The writing is precise, direct, and invites one to keep reading. It is consistent and very clear."
Joan Fleet
Counselling and Career Development Services
University of Western Ontario

"Who is this person? Can I meet them and shake their hand? The nail was hit on the head so many times, I think we've built a house! *Transitions: It's Your Education* is very realistic, down to earth, and it centers around you, the individual. I can't stress how realistic it is; it's so refreshing."
Joanne Cheverie
Student
University of Prince Edward Island

"*Power over Time: Student Success with Time Management* is an excellent book for students and does indeed fill a void in the current market. Time management is a crucial skill for student success, and a transferable job skill that is requisite for success in the occupational world as well. Good time management assists in alleviating and controlling stress, factors which are covered in this text."
Brooke White
Professor
University of Windsor

"I am not aware of any books which deal with time mangement as thoroughly as [does] *Power over Time: Student Success with Time Management*."
Laurie Taschuk
Professor
Grant MacEwan College

PREFACE

Students can be excellent teachers. It is through our daily interactions with students, as learning skills counsellors at The University of Western Ontario, that we have gathered a wealth of practical information about time management as it relates to the academic experience. Many students have contributed directly to this book. In it you will see reflections of the habits and concerns of actual students. For example, the case studies used throughout *Power over Time* are based on real experiences reported by students. What this means is that the time management principles and strategies presented here have been tested in the field. Students have applied the principles and reported on their effectiveness. In many cases, the "tips" on time management originated directly from students themselves.

In our experience, students who are successful demonstrate strong time management skills. This realization is not a secret. At some point in their academic careers, a large number of students recognize the importance of time management and seek out help with time management problems. This book is a practical guide to effective time management. It offers a self-help resource for students, as well as a useful tool for teachers and counsellors who work with students. The goals of this book are to:

- *encourage reflection and self assessment by the reader*
- *explore issues of time management from a broad and varied perspective*
- *present a range of ideas useful to the reader who is seeking specific time management strategies*
- *facilitate sound decision making which can lead to positive changes in the time management behaviour of students.*

To reach these goals this book employs a variety of means: text, assessment inventories, problem-based case studies, and worksheets. Attainment of these goals, however, hinges on each student's commitment to improve his or her own approach to time management. We hope that this book will help students to make the most of their learning experiences by contributing to academic success through effective time management.

Joan Fleet and Denise Reaume
London, Ontario

ACKNOWLEDGEMENTS

The authors and publisher would like to thank the following reviewers for their fine contributions to the development of this book: Shirley Henderson, Carol Potter, Laurie Taschuk, and Brooke White.

ABOUT THE HARBRACE GUIDES TO STUDENT SUCCESS SERIES

A series of accessible, affordable, and practical books, the HARBRACE GUIDES TO STUDENT SUCCESS are dedicated to fostering student success in all its diversity. Books now available in the series are listed on the flyleaf. Look for forthcoming titles on dealing with stress, managing your time, managing your finances, and exam success.

A NOTE FROM THE PUBLISHER

Thank you for selecting *Power over Time: Student Success with Time Management* by Joan Fleet and Denise Reaume. The authors and publisher have devoted considerable time to the careful development of this book. We appreciate your recognition of this effort and accomplishment.

We want to hear what you think about *Power over Time: Student Success with Time Management*. Please take a few minutes to fill in the stamped reply card at the back of the book. Your comments and suggestions will be valuable to us as we prepare new editions and other books.

CONTENTS

Chapter 1

YOU AND TIME

FIRST THINGS FIRST

▷ Hello There!

This book, *Power over Time: Student Success with Time Management*, has been especially written for students studying in colleges, universities, and in the senior grades of high school. It is a book for people who have to make a lot of decisions about time, and it recognizes the special challenges that students face as they try to juggle and balance all of the varying demands of school and non-school activities. Because of modern trends in education, the group for whom the book is written is very broad indeed. It covers the whole spectrum from young adults to seniors. If you are in school, wish to develop better time management skills, and are in the 16 to 80 age group -- then this book is for you!

Throughout this book there will be many opportunities for you to reflect on your own experience with time management, to respond to questions, complete worksheets and pose solutions for case studies. Working interactively with the text will allow you to explore your own personal approach to time management, identifying your strengths and pinpointing any weaknesses. By taking an active role as you read, you will be able to put into practice more quickly those time management techniques that best suit your needs.

This first chapter explores general issues related to your own time management. Because you are taking the time to read this book, it is fairly safe to assume that you are not totally satisfied with the time management techniques that you currently use. This may be for any number of reasons. For example, typical situations that present time management problems for students, and with which you may identify, include:

* *Moving to a different grade or to a new school*
* *Having too little time available for all the study tasks that need to be done*
* *Trying to "catch up" after a spell of procrastination*
* *Finding a reasonable balance between studying and recreational activities, such as sports, watching TV or spending time with friends*
* *Coping with school as well as with a full or part-time job and/or family responsibilities*

Before you read further, take a little time to think about yourself as a student. **What are the current time issues for you?** If you wish to develop skills you need to think about the challenges that you face.

Current time management issues for me include:

_____

_____

_____

_____

_____

_____

_____

TAKING A CLOSE LOOK AT TIME

▷ **How Much Time?**

Whichever way we look at it, we can't stretch the amount of time we have. A student, looking through her day planner, exclaimed, *"If I could just add two more blank pages in here everything would be alright."* It is a sure bet that few students would turn down the opportunity of two extra weeks somewhere in the middle of a busy term, but reality tells us that we do not have that luxury. We all have the same amount of time:

✓ 60 minutes per hour
✓ 24 hours per day
✓ 7 days per week
✓ 52 weeks per year

It is an interesting thought that each one of us has the same number of hours in each day as the world's outstanding people. Journalists, film makers, rock musicians, business leaders, national politicians, researchers -- all lead their lives within the constraints of a 24 hour day. You might say, "*Well it's easy for them. They have managers and secretaries and other support staff.*" However, it is most likely that they were and are very motivated to make the most of the time that is available to them. It is also likely that they follow some rules about what they can and cannot accomplish within the constraints that time imposes. Ask yourself the question, "**Are there enough hours in the day for what I wish to accomplish?**"

▷ Choices?

We all have choices when it comes to time. You are a student and so your choices reflect a student lifestyle. You attend classes, complete assignments, read and review materials to prepare for class, and prepare for tests. To do a good job as a student you have to commit a reasonable amount of time to those activities.

In addition, there are so many other activities that are part of your life and finding time for everything is the big challenge. It is easy to get over-involved in activities or to set unrealistic expectations given all of your commitments. Each one of us has to make choices about what we can and cannot do, given our personal goals. Take a look at some interesting people and think about the choices that face them as they try to manage their time effectively. **How similar are their choices to your own?**

PETER: *Peter is in his final year of high school. He volunteered to be editor of the yearbook and it is taking far more time than he expected. He has a part-time job three nights a week because his family is not in a position to assist him financially with school. He has set high standards for his school work as he is applying to university.*

LEE: *Lee is attending community college in his home town. He is in the library technician programme which integrates class time with on-the-job placements that can last up to three months. Lee has to plan carefully because he has to drop off his daughter at the baby sitter's each day. He tends to worry about written assignments as they can take a lot of time for research and writing, cutting down on his time with the family.*

SABINE: *Sabine is in her third year of a degree programme in chemistry. She likes to swim several times a week and she is on a residence basketball team. She volunteers for three hours a week at the local elementary school. This year she is taking an optional course in advanced math and it is proving to be quite a challenge.*

KERRY: *Kerry is a graduate student in psychology. She is finishing the last of her experimental work and beginning to organize writing her thesis. She also is teaching a first-year undergraduate course and lecture preparation is time consuming. She spends a lot of time at the drop-in help centre with students.*

▷ **Your Current Skills**

Most students know a lot about time management techniques but may, at the same time, have a hard time putting techniques into practice. Think about that for a moment. **What do you know about the way in which effective people manage time?** Imagine that everyone knows that you are a great time manager. A journalist for the student newspaper asks if you can give some tips to the incoming students to help them get on track early with time management. You may be surprised at the sound advice you can offer others.

My time management tips for incoming students are:

_____

_____

_____

_____

_____

_____

▷ **Bad Habits Anyone?**

Some people will be reading this book because they know that they have developed bad habits around time management and are having difficulty changing their behaviour. A few may have really major problems -- like the student who spent almost a whole year in the games room at school playing video games. Even though this student loved his program and had a clear career goal, he had a very difficult time getting down to work. The excitement of the video machines was too compelling.

Much more commonly, however, poor habits are less dramatic but nonetheless frustrating. **Do you identify with some of the following common problems?** You may find yourself switching on the TV when you know you have work to do. You may tidy your desk or wash dishes and know that these are not high priority activities. You may daydream as you try to study. You may find yourself raiding the fridge or making a cup of coffee many times each study session. If this describes your own experience, then you have much in common with many other students. These are the kind of behaviours that can get in the way of effective time management and are often resistant to change.

▷ **Too Much to Do?**

Some people will be reading this book because, rather than being procrastinators, they overwork and yet still feel dissatisfied with their accomplishments. For example, a student who had been valedictorian at his high school, and who did not want to let his high school teachers down now that he was at university, was working almost all of the time. He was allowing himself only four hours of sleep a night (3:00 - 7:00 a.m.). He dared not make choices about what to study and so covered absolutely everything. If a student works this way and then experiences some negative results, motivation can become a real issue. *"I worked so hard for that test and I could not believe the mark I got. I haven't been able to do anything since I got it back."* Such students seem to get trapped in an "all or nothing" syndrome.

One medical student was very frustrated because she was putting in hours and hours of time memorising information in courses such as anatomy, histology and physiology but her marks did not reflect the effort. *"I have to find a different approach,"* she said, *"because I realise that I am having absolutely no fun or social life and yet, at the same time, my marks are not good."* This insight was the first step in her determining a more efficient study approach that led to improved marks and personal satisfaction. **Do you feel overwhelmed by school work?**

> ### Changing Behaviour

Sometimes, something happens to make a student take stock and decide to change the way in which time is managed. It might be that, as in the case of the student who spent time playing video games, the student fails a course or programme and is therefore faced with very negative consequences of personal actions. In more typical scenarios, students may feel that marks, although adequate, are far below potential. Feelings of low self esteem and frustration about self-defeating behaviours are typically behind decisions to manage time more efficiently. Students are often well aware of the cumulative effects of many minor instances of procrastination and/or poor concentration. On the other hand, there are many students who, rather than doing too little work, find themselves, like the medical student, working all of the time. These examples illustrate typical students who, for different reasons, are faced with making choices about changing some fundamental time management behaviours.

Students who recognize that they are dissatisfied with the way in which they currently manage time are faced with a choice. They can continue to let time happen in the same old way or they can make conscious decisions to manage time actively by setting new personal goals and working towards them. Maintaining the status quo and letting time happen in old patterns may seem to be a more comfortable approach, as it requires so little effort. It may also be viewed by a student to be a more spontaneous approach and less controlled by the demands of society. For some students, that is the great attraction of the *"just let it happen in the same old way"* mode. It takes more active effort to move in new directions to managing time, but it can result in very positive changes.

Established behaviour patterns are not easy to change and time management is no exception. Old habits die hard. We all know about New Year's resolutions! Much of what we do each day is done fairly automatically. Things are completed in our usual way almost before we realise that we have acted. At the same time, overall behaviour patterns do evolve slowly and continuously, so that we may not even notice that they have changed until we look back and realise that we are doing things differently. There are, also, times when change takes place rapidly, when we feel strongly enough about the need for change that we can make considerable progress over a short period of time. If motivation is high, considerable development of our time management behaviour is possible. **Is this a time in your own academic experience to recognise the need to change old habits or develop new skills, and to try some new approaches to your own time management?**

▷ **So Where Shall I Begin?**

There are two important early steps necessary to the development of effective time management. The first step is to take a close look at the way you currently manage time. The second step is to set some initial goals for change.

1.   *Self Assessment*

Self assessment of your study time patterns allows you to explore and evaluate the range of decisions you make each day with regard to time management. Managing time is a very complex process and self assessment provides some measures of your strengths and weaknesses.

2.   *Initial Goals*

After you have completed the assessment of your study-time patterns, you will be asked to *select five items* from the inventory that you feel are weaknesses for you and are high on your priority list for change. It is important when developing new skills that you work to develop only a few new skills at any one time. Change needs focus. As you continue to read through this book, there will be many opportunities to explore ways of reaching these important initial goals.

SELF ASSESSMENT

▷ **Study-Time Patterns**

Do these items reflect you as a student? No Y

1.	I keep a careful record of the dates of upcoming major events such as tests and assignments.	1 2 3 4 5
2.	I often feel really panicky about being behind with my work.	1 2 3 4 5
3.	During a study session, I set small goals and work to achieve them (e.g., read 5 pages of text and do 3 math problems).	1 2 3 4 5
4.	I tend to miss classes.	1 2 3 4 5
5.	If I need to solve a problem quickly, I get help from another student, the teacher, or other help resources.	1 2 3 4 5
6.	I often miscalculate how much time homework tasks will take.	1 2 3 4 5
7.	I have set up a regular plan for my study activities.	1 2 3 4 5
8.	I find my current course load too heavy.	1 2 3 4 5
9.	I begin assignments early so that I will have time to do a good job.	1 2 3 4 5
10.	I have difficulty concentrating while doing homework.	1 2 3 4 5

11. I plan ahead so I can be flexible about putting in extra hours if I have a lot of school work to do.   1 2 3 4 5

12. I always seem to be behind with my work.   1 2 3 4 5

13. I regularly use a day planner to plan my activities.   1 2 3 4 5

14. My marks tend to suffer because of last minute cramming for tests.   1 2 3 4 5

15. Each day I have clear goals of what I wish to accomplish.   1 2 3 4 5

16. I am easily distracted from school work by my friends, TV, etc.   1 2 3 4 5

17. I really enjoy working on the courses I am taking.   1 2 3 4 5

18. I can only work if I feel like working.   1 2 3 4 5

19. I prioritise tasks effectively.   1 2 3 4 5

20. I have a hard time deciding just what school work I should be doing outside class.   1 2 3 4 5

▷ **Scoring the Inventory**

Your score for each item										Total
1	3	5	7	9	11	13	15	17	19	
2	4	6	8	10	12	14	16	18	20	
Total for ODD numbers minus total for EVEN numbers =										

Odd-numbered items in the inventory reflect positive components of time management that can contribute to effective use of time. Even-numbered items reflect negative components that can take away from effective time management. Therefore, if you have a positive total score, this indicates a proactive approach to managing time. If your score is negative, your time management strategies can be improved. However, remember that there is not one right way to manage time. You need to find the right approach for you that will allow for tasks to be completed on time, without necessitating superhuman effort. It will also ensure that your stress level is reasonable.[1]

---

[1]See Appendix A for more detailed discussion of the inventory

INITIAL GOALS

Look back to your completed self assessment of study-time patterns. Of the twenty items on the inventory, *select five items* that you feel are important time management issues for you. These may be typical behaviours that are currently detracting from your personal satisfaction and potential performance as a student. **What would you like to change for the better?** As you read and work through the book you will be able to evaluate many suggestions that will enable you to reach these important initial goals.

My initial goals for time management are to work on:

1._____

2._____

3._____

4._____

5._____

QUESTIONS FOR REFLECTION

- *What are current time management issues for you?*
- *What are your hardest choices as you combine academic and non-academic activities?*
- *What effective time management techniques do you know about, and yet not currently use yourself?*
- *Do you have any consistent bad habits with time management and, if so, what are they?*
- *Do you have a very heavy workload and, if so, have you thought of any ways to handle it?*
- *Do you "manage" time or do you "let it happen?"*
- *What insights into your time management behaviour did you gain from self assessment of study patterns?*
- *What initial goals have you set for yourself?*

Chapter 2

THE CHALLENGE OF TIME MANAGEMENT

PEOPLE AND TIME

▷ *A Common Challenge*

▷ *Success Stories*

▷ *Common Themes*

▷ *Learning from Experience*

JUST FOR STUDENTS

▷ *Problems and Myths Affecting Time Management for Students*

▷ *Time Management Tips*

QUESTIONS FOR REFLECTION

PEOPLE AND TIME

▷ A Common Challenge

Life for a student can be very busy. There are classes to attend, reading and studying, and assignments to complete. In addition, there are usually many opportunities to be involved in extra-curricular activities and, of course, there are also family and friends with whom to spend time. Finding time for everything is not an easy task.

Chapter One, "*You and Time*," explored some initial aspects of your own experience with time. Now this chapter on "*The Challenge of Time Management*" looks at the way in which we can learn about time management from other people. The way in which we learn from those around us is often referred to as "*observational learning*" and when teachers or individuals teach others by demonstrating to them the tasks they have to complete, we call that style of teaching "*modelling.*"

Because we are exploring the characteristics of effective time management behaviour, this chapter first of all looks at the experience of successful Canadians. Secondly, it looks at problems with time management that are commonly reported by students. Managing time well is a challenge shared by people from all walks of life and, because much of our own learning takes place through observing the behaviour of others, it is important to evaluate what we see happening around us. Effective approaches to time management are often visible, so we can observe the way in which good time managers operate.

▷ Success Stories

Some people really stand out from the crowd. They are the people who are at the top of their respective fields and who show leadership in the way in which they live their lives. Few people get to the top without a great deal of hard work and goals to guide their time management. We can learn a lot from the way in which successful people manage their time. Although we, ourselves, may or may not reach the same degree of prominence in society, we can all work toward our own definition of success.

We asked some prominent Canadians about their success. We wanted to know about specific time management strategies that they identified as contributing to their success. They were generous in their responses and contributed ideas for your consideration. As you read through their contributions, look for specific suggestions that they make. In the space in the margin make a note of any strategies that they mention and watch for any recurrent themes. Although these Canadians are all from different walks of life, they share the common challenge of managing time.

> **EDWIN MIRVISH**
> *Entrepreneur and*
> *Patron of the Arts*

Ever since I started working at nine years of age (almost 70 years ago) I have always been paranoid about time! I have always felt that, next to good health, time is our most valuable possession. My watch is always set ten minutes ahead of time. Someone once said that people who are early for appointments have an "anxiety complex." People who are always exactly on time for an appointment are "compulsive." People who are always late for appointments have "hostility." Almost without exception I am usually early for my appointments. I not only have great appreciation for my own time, but I also have great respect for the time of others.

Ever since my youth I have always felt that there was so much to do and so little time in which to do it. Today, at 79 years of age, I still begin my day at Honest Ed's retail store at 8 a.m. I absolutely cannot move without my watch. I am naked without it. My personal advice to students is that they should have great respect and thoughtfulness in the way they use their time.

Time has its way of slipping past. To me there is nothing sadder than to see someone in their middle years look back and wonder where and how their past years have gone. I can only speak from my personal feelings and needs. On the other hand there are probably many people in this world who have had a life of fun, fun, fun. These people would probably not trade places with me under any conditions. Who am I to say they are wrong? Fortunately we live in a country where each of us has the opportunity to express ourselves in our own creative, individual way.

"Time" is a most precious gift. I want to make every moment as productive as I can.

RICK HANSEN
National Fellow - Disabilities
University of British Columbia

A very important time management strategy for me is to manage myself as opposed to having my schedule manage me. I would advise students to identify their priorities, determine the amount of time they are prepared to spend on those priorities, monitor their progress to ensure that they are sticking to their original aims, and allow themselves the flexibility to adapt and to change, just as life for all of us changes.

Time management was one of the keys to my success because it allowed me to become more efficient in the use of my time, and it ensures that "I walk my talk."

My time management advice to students in high school and post-secondary education is to manage time from the inside out, based on personal principles, objectives and goals. These must be the guidelines which govern their actions and activities.

In addition, I would like to make the following comment about time management. To be an effective and empowered individual one must make the best use of one's time on this earth. Doing our personal best, having a focused strategy, and being well organised allows us to be the best we can be with what we have, and to reach our full potential.

LINCOLN ALEXANDER
24th Lieutenant Governor
of Ontario

My success, if any, comes as a result of believing in myself, setting goals, and being obsessed with mental and physical work to the extreme in order to understand and overcome all challenges of the goals. I, at all times, tried my best to be the best.

THALIA ASSURAS
Television Journalist

A very important time management strategy for me is writing lists and keeping to an agenda and timetable that I organize at the beginning of every week, sometimes at the beginning of every day. One of the most important factors is keeping oneself to deadlines and not procrastinating about procrastinating.

Time is of the essence in journalism where so much is measured in time periods. Writing tightly and concisely and interviewing in the same manner produce the desired result.

My advice to students in high school and post-secondary education is to try to do what you have to do on time, instead of procrastinating (not always possible, I know). That avoids anxiety and helps you to overcome unforeseen obstacles.

But also remember that if you can't manage your time well, all of the time, don't be too hard on yourself. You're only human!

▷ **Common Themes**

Now that you have gained some insight into time management strategies of successful Canadians, think about the similarities and differences among them. **What do you think are typical time management strategies related to success?**

_____

_____

_____

_____

_____

_____

_____

▷ Learning from Experience

One of the most powerful ways of learning is through observing the behaviour of other people and interacting with them. The way in which one person manages time has a significant impact on those with whom that person is in close contact. For example, if you live or work with someone who is very organised and goal oriented, you may reap some of the benefits from that effective time management behaviour, both from improving your own time management strategies and from your own environment being a more organised place in which to operate. On the other hand, it can be very frustrating if someone is always late, disorganised, and cannot deliver work on time. As you read through the following descriptions, think how you would interact with each person. **What would you learn from the experience and, in particular, what would be the positive and negative aspects, for you, of the ways in which they manage time?**

"My friend is really easy to be around. She is always so laid back. Nothing seems to pressure her and yet she always seems to get things done. I think that she is pretty well organised and she has a good sense of how much she can handle."

"I know this one student who is a disaster! He never goes to bed until the early hours of the morning and then he can't get up until noon. He must have missed at least half his classes. He tends to squeak by depending on friends to bail him out by providing class notes."

"There's this person in my lab class. She is super organised and has everything planned to the last minute. There is no time for the unexpected. I often feel that she is so efficient that reasonable alternatives are not fully explored and creative solutions missed."

_____

_____

_____

_____

_____

_____

JUST FOR STUDENTS

▷ Problems and Myths Affecting Time Management for Students

Many problems that students typically report have associated time management implications, and can take on exaggerated personal significance if accompanied by myths about a student's ability to handle these problems. For example, a myth for many students is the one that says, *"If I spend all of my time studying and do nothing but school work, I will get high marks."* This is a myth that says that quantity of work leads to quality performance. While it is important to spend a reasonable amount of time regularly on study activities, it is much more important to be a strategic learner and to find effective ways of learning that lead to a sound understanding of the course content.

As you read through the commonly reported problems, ask yourself, **"Do I experience any of these problems? Do I believe these myths?"**

Problem # 1 Finding enough study time for each course

x ✓   *"I should have enough time to study everything and get high marks."*

A single parent of three children, who had to commute 40 kilometres to school, had a part-time job and who was taking three courses, was disappointed because she was not getting "A" grades! She simply did not have the time necessary for achieving the goals that she had set for herself. As courses become more demanding, a student needs enough time to understand new ideas, consolidate information, and apply information to new situations. Teachers can place high demands on the student and overload can occur. If the student is to survive, he or she needs to find ways of prioritising activities so that the required tasks can get done within a reasonable schedule. If that is impossible, a re-evaluation of academic goals may suggest that a lighter course load is necessary.

Problem # 2 Lacking direction about out-of-class study tasks

x ✓   *"I should know, intuitively, what learning activities will help me to learn this."*

As students progress through the educational system they assume more and more of the responsibility for managing their own learning. This means that by the time a student is at college or university, instructions about many of the "homework" activities may be vague or non existent. A student may not make good choices about the kinds of activities that result in efficient handling of the concepts. It sometimes requires trial and error before the best approach is found. If a student continues to experience problems, a talk with a teacher, another student, or a learning skills counsellor may get that student on the right track.

Problem # 3 Living with a competitive atmosphere in class

x ✓ *"My class mates should be there for me if I need help."*

Some students are very competitive for top marks and, therefore, not always very cooperative. Commonly, higher marks open doors. These doors may lead to scholarships or placement in limited enrolment programs, to positions in school organisations, and better access to jobs. Therefore, in some educational settings there can be a real climate of competitive over cooperative learning. This can result in students not sharing information as readily as they might, and therefore reducing informal peer support available to the group as a whole. On the other hand, there are always students who do not subscribe to heavy competition and who are only too ready to help others. You may or may not agree with a competitive learning environment. It is important to find the niche that is right for you, where you can learn effectively and where the level of competition allows for your own best performance.

Problem # 4 Being uncertain about your career goals

x ✓ *"I should know what kind of job I hope to be doing after graduation."*

There can be a lot of pressure, especially from close friends or family, for a student to know exactly what he or she wants to do in life. *"What do you want to be? What kind of a job do you expect to get?"* These are very difficult questions to answer for many students. Although some students are quite happy not knowing precise details about their future, for others this can be a worrying situation. Career questions and concerns may have considerable impact on motivation and, consequently, on time management. If this is an issue for you, explore the career services of your school. By clarifying goals you can put your current course work into clearer perspective.

Problem # 5 Combining paid employment with the student experience

x ✓ *"I should be able to work part time without affecting my grades."*

For many students a part-time job is a fact of life. It is the only way that they can afford to stay in school. One high school student was working 35 hours at the local corner store, including two full-night shifts on the weekend and, at the same time, carrying a full load of academic courses. His academic performance was not great! Typical fallout from unrealistic job demands is tiredness and lack of time and motivation to do homework. It is important to be realistic about the balance of work at school and on the job. If working at a job outside school is the only way you can afford to be in school, you will have to make sound decisions on the course load you can handle. Only you can draw the line on your own energy to work effectively.

Problem # 6 Balancing time for important relationships with time for studying

x ✓ *"I should be able to handle school and spend a lot of time with my partner."*

School is often a great place to meet new friends, to develop close relationships, and even to fall in love! Commitment to a relationship can require considerable time together. A student in love may not find it easy to get that other person out of mind, and poor concentration can be a great time waster. Relationships are a crucial part of life and if we are to have the best of both worlds -- meaningful relationships and successful academic experience -- this needs a lot of proactive time management planning. Plan for the times that you wish to spend with friends. Planning does not necessarily need to be rigid; it can leave room for spontaneity. However, if you do not plan at all, you will find that socialising can take up an unreasonable amount of your available time.

Problem # 7 Adjusting to living away from home

x ✓ *"Life at school, in a new city and away from home, should be a lot of fun."*

For the traditional student leaving home for the first time, adapting to life without the family can be an enormous adjustment. Although this can be a welcomed and positive change and a very natural step to greater autonomy, it does not always work out this way. Some students may spend a lot of time thinking about people, places or experiences they miss. Homesickness can be devastating. It can affect anyone: the mature student relocating away from family and friends or the graduate student moving on to a new institution. In all of these cases the student has to find ways of handling the crisis without jeopardising his or her academic future. It is the first year experience that can be the most difficult for many students. It can take time to meet people with whom you feel comfortable. It is not easy and may require some informal or formal counselling to overcome the problem.

Problem # 8 Understanding the relationship between effort and marks

x ✓ *"All I need to do to get better marks is to spend more time studying."*

Although good performance is certainly linked to commitment to study, higher and higher grades will not necessarily result from more and more work. One very angry and frustrated student pointed to a "C" grade on an essay and said, *"I put hours of work into that paper. It definitely deserved a higher grade than that."* A high mark usually points to more than putting in time. It also indicates a high level of comprehension, interpretation of the assignment and creative input. If you are not happy with a grade, you may need to ask the teacher to go over a returned test or assignment with you. This will help to identify the problem and to find ways of improving future performance.

Problem # 9 Finding a quiet place to study

x ✓   *"My roommates should be more thoughtful. It is so noisy and I am constantly interrupted."*

Finding a place to work that allows for full concentration is important for efficient learning. Efficient academic work allows for more time to be available for other activities. Working hard and playing hard is the best of both worlds! There are always locations where work happens and, also, places which sabotage a good work effort. Students often have to share space with others. These may be other family members for those students who live at home. It might be a roommate, or a graduate student sharing office space.

You have to take charge of your study location, either by relocating somewhere quieter or by negotiating with those with whom you share space. One mature student had four young children. His solution worked! *"I bought a very bright red hat"* he said,*"that I called my 'study' hat. When I had it on, the children could not talk to me. When it was off, though, we could play and have lots of fun together."* It was a solution that was appropriate for the situation. Sharing space with others requires compromise -- hopefully on both sides! Try to find a location or negotiate a situation that will allow you to engage in high quality study time.

It is a good idea to explore a variety of different work locations. There may be a number of libraries or work rooms that provide just the right conditions for the study tasks you need to accomplish. Working only in your own room can be very limiting, unless you feel confident that it always produces the highest levels of concentration.

▷ **Time Management Tips**

Successful students are very often the best time managers. They tend to be involved in much more than just academic work and are able to achieve a balance between studying and other activities. Here are some of the favourite time management tips from successful senior students. **Which of the following would work best for you?**

✓ **Set your priorities**

Stephen: "*I'm really having a good time at university. I'm learning interesting things and meeting some great people, but sometimes those great people try to persuade me to do things other than study and sometimes it's hard to say no. Before I give in and say yes, I stop myself and remember why I'm at university and think about the academic goals I have set for myself. Having a good time is important, but I try to remind myself daily that I am at university to learn. My education is my first priority.*"

✓ **Reward yourself for working hard**

Pam: "*Every week I try really hard to get all of my work done by Saturday night so I can reward myself by taking Sunday off. Being able to have one day in seven when I could do exactly what I want -- sleep all day, go for a long bike ride or just stay home and pet the cat -- gives me great incentive to get all of my work done in six days.*"

✓ **Use small blocks of time**

Pat: "*When I have an hour between classes during the day, I use the time to go to the library and get some of my reserved readings done or I look over my notes from my previous class instead of going to the Games Room to shoot a game of pool. It's too easy to be in the middle of a game when my next class begins, so I always try to leave pool-playing until the end of the day.*"

✓ **Try it for five minutes**

Lex: "*Even if it's a subject I absolutely hate but I know I have to study for, I promise myself to work on it for just five minutes. If I'm not into it in five minutes I quit and put it aside to try it again later, but I usually find that five minutes stretches very easily and becomes a half an hour or more.*"

✓ **Always go to class**

Kim: "*Last year I wasn't always the greatest at being prepared for class, but I always went. By never missing a class I always knew what was going on and what was expected of me. I didn't get too far behind, even if I didn't have the chapter read or all of my assignments finished.*"

✓ Beware of TV

Lindsay: "*I make deals with myself, especially about TV shows. I choose which ones I am going to watch and I watch and enjoy them. Otherwise I don't switch it on.*"

✓ Find a good place to study

Tim: "*I like listening to music, so when I study I find a quiet corner lounge and listen to one of my favourite tapes with my walkman. The music blocks out all other noises and the tape lasts 45 minutes, just long enough to justify taking a 15 minute break. Studying, for me, is a lot easier when I'm in a comfortable environment. I mean, it's got to be done so I try to make it as painless as possible.*"

✓ Take action against distractions

Carla: "*I can get easily distracted by what other people are doing. If they watch TV then I will too. The only way for me is to get away from the distractions where I can work - - like the library.*"

✓ Do "catch up" if necessary

Michelle: "*If I find myself procrastinating, I'll plan extra time and do some catching up before things get out of hand.*"

QUESTIONS FOR REFLECTION

- *What are the most common time management problems for people in general?*
- *What are the most typical time management strategies of successful people?*
- *Which of the typical problems and myths discussed in this chapter best reflected your own problems with time management?*
- *What characteristics do you look for in a good model for time management?*
- *What time management strategies do you regard as being most effective?*

## Chapter 3

TIME MANAGEMENT PRINCIPLES

KEYS TO SUCCESS

A POT-POURRI OF PRINCIPLES

- ▷ *Set Academic Goals*
- ▷ *Plan Ahead and Record Important Events*
- ▷ *Locate Useful Resources*
- ▷ *Find and Use a Good Work Location*
- ▷ *Know and Use your "Best Times"*
- ▷ *Make "to do"Lists*
- ▷ *Flag Start Dates*
- ▷ *Subdivide One Large Task into Many Smaller Tasks*
- ▷ *Plan Each Day*
- ▷ *Engage in Time-Saving Tasks*
- ▷ *Be Flexible*
- ▷ *Evaluate Your Progress*

WHAT'S YOUR CHOICE?

CASE STUDY FOR REFLECTION

KEYS TO SUCCESS

Effective time management systems are based on **time management principles**. Sometimes, applying just one positive time management principle consistently can make all the difference between being efficient or inefficient as a manager of time. For example, one student who also had a part-time job in a busy administrative office was asked how she handled so much paper work in the office. Her response was, "*If at all possible, I never touch a piece of paper twice. For example, when I open the mail I immediately answer it, pass it on to someone else, record the information if necessary, or put it in the garbage!*" By consistently applying the positive time management principle of **"do it now"**, the student was saving herself a lot of time and worry. This is in contrast to the negative principle of **"I'll do it later"** which, if consistently applied, results in a massive backlog of work or lost opportunities because important deadlines are missed.

If you were to ask half a dozen of your friends how they managed their time as students, you would not expect all of their replies to be exactly the same. Although there might be some similarities, each friend would approach time management in a way that matched his or her own personal style, goals and needs. One of the keys to your success as a student is a time management system that is just right for you. Your system should enable you to handle the busy academic and social demands of school. It should be a flexible system allowing for variety in the school year. There will be some weeks when you can take a more relaxed approach to your studies; there will also be weeks which will demand a very disciplined approach to your studies.

You will find, at different times in the academic year, that you apply different time management principles depending on current needs. This chapter introduces time management principles that can contribute to student success. In this chapter, these time management principles are introduced for your consideration. In Chapter Four, "*Your Action Plan,*" you will apply the principles as you design your own time management system. As you evaluate each one of the time management principles, ask yourself these questions:

"*Is this principle one that is already part of my time management system?*"

"*Is this principle familiar to me but one that I rarely think about or apply?*"

"*Is this a new idea that I can build into my own time management system?*"

"*At what time in the school year would I need to think about, or apply, this principle?*"

A POT-POURRI OF PRINCIPLES

▷ Set Academic Goals

If you set clear academic goals you will find that it is easier to stay motivated to do school work, even when the going gets tough. Some of your goals will relate to your future career, future educational plans, your current programme of study, as well as to the day-to-day completion of study tasks. Celeste and Alex are typical students talking about the variety of goals that help to motivate them as students.

CELESTE: *In my first year of school I was not sure what I wanted to do with my life but, as I like being in school, I was content just to be here and to take a variety of first year courses. I especially enjoyed my politics class and so chose to major in honours politics. After graduation I may apply to teacher's college, but Law is another option right now. I can leave my options open until next year. This week, though, the most important goals I have are finishing a major paper and studying for a mid-term test. Right now I am off to the library to find an important article for my paper.*

ALEX: *I've always wanted to own my own garage and the auto mechanics course in college seemed a good place to start. I have found this first year to be a heavy load but I am determined to stick with it as I have been promised a summer job in the garage where I did my job placement. I know that it may take a while but I am sure that I'll get my own business some day. This week my goal is to get a big project finished in shop. We've just about rebuilt an old engine and I should be able to finish it by tomorrow. I want to get it finished so that I can get down to studying for exams.*

Academic goals are important to continuing motivation to do work, but it is not always possible to know exactly where your studies will lead. Alex has a more definite plan for the future than does Celeste. He knows that he wants to own his own garage, but Celeste has two options that she is considering. It is a good idea to have a back up plan in case things do not go as planned. Students who set very rigid (and often very high) goals may be disappointed if they do not get the marks they need to reach those goals. Alex and Celeste both have clear short-term goals, and it is the day-to-day plans that direct work that are most responsible for success.

▷ Plan Ahead and Record Important Events

One of the frustrating, but very typical, aspects of academic life is that, often, deadlines all arrive together. There may be one week, especially around the middle of the term, when you have several essays to hand in as well as having to write a number of mid-term tests. If you have not planned ahead for such a situation then you may have a very real problem. It is not uncommon for a student to get very over tired, panicky, and even to get physically ill if he or she is swamped with work over a very short period of time.

If you want to keep deadlines under control, it is important to have a system for recording important academic test dates and assignment due dates. It is also just as important to record important personal or social events that will take additional time away from studying. Your system for recording should be very easy to access, so that you are reminded frequently of these upcoming major events. Many students use a wall calendar above or on their desks. A calendar should be chosen that allows space for writing in the events for each day. It is also useful to be able to see at least one whole month at a glance. It is a good idea to record important dates in more than one way, for example, also in a day planner or on a weekly time table. In Chapter Four, *"Your Action Plan"*, there are examples of worksheets that will allow you to plan ahead. You will also find extra copies of these organizers in APPENDIX B.

▷ Locate Useful Resources

If you want to make the best use of your time you will want to know those people and places that can be useful resources if you need them. The obvious resource for a student is the teacher. As you leave high school and move on to post-secondary education you will find that classes are generally much larger and you have less personal contact with teachers. It is not uncommon for the teachers to set "office hours" for students in their classes. You can meet with a teacher during office hours to discuss any problems that you may be experiencing. You need to be aware of the times at which the teacher is available and if there is a conflict with your own schedule you may be able to arrange an alternate time.

In a more informal way, other students can also be a sound resource. If you can make contact with a classmate or student who is proficient with the course you may find that he or she can help clarify important concepts with which you may be experiencing problems.

Schools, colleges and universities usually provide many other support resources. If students are good consumers of these services, this can make learning an efficient activity. Services can range from "help centres" for key courses, tutorial services, typing, computing and photocopying services, to counselling and library services. You should explore the resources that are available to you so that when you need to use them you know where they are located and times when they are available.

▷ Find and Use a Good Work Location

One of the greatest time wasters for students is poor concentration. Students report that they spend too much time daydreaming or looking around to check out what is going on around them. It is very important to find a work location, or combination of work locations, in which you can concentrate and get work done. You know that you have an efficient system when you can both work hard and play hard. That is, when you spend time studying you should get through a reasonable quantity of work, without wasting too much time. Then you feel good about spending time with friends or in other activities of your choice.

Effective work locations are specific to the individual. You will know what type of location works for you. Maybe it is the library or a study room in school or residence. It might be your own room or even the kitchen table in the middle of a busy house. Some students require absolute silence while others like some noise and activity going on around them. You will have to make the right choice for yourself.

▷ Know and Use your "*Best Times*"

Are you an "*early morning person*", a "*daytimer*", "*evenings only*", a "*midnight owl*" or a little bit of all four? The "*early morning person*" is alert as soon as he or she wakes in the morning and can get down to work between 6:00 and 8:00 a.m.. "*Daytimers*" are your regular 9:00 a.m. to 5:00 p.m. people. They like to make full use of hours in between classes so that when they go home or back to residence they can spend most of the time relaxing. Perhaps the most common work pattern of all is that of the "*evenings only*" crowd. They get their best work done between 7:00 and 11:00 p.m. Then there are "*night owls*" who only get going around 10:00 p.m. when others around them may be thinking of going to bed. In the quiet, early hours of the morning the "*night owls*" are working away.

Only you can judge the time of day at which you are most mentally alert. If you can make good use of your "*best times*", you can work most efficiently. If you claim to be a "*night owl*", think carefully about your reasons for establishing this pattern. Many students fall into this pattern because they have a problem dealing with distractions. When everyone else is sleeping, many of the distractions are removed. You may need to rethink your management of non-studying activities.

▷ Make "*to do*" Lists

When you write a list of tasks that you wish to complete you achieve three very important goals. The first is that you track what has to be done. As you think about your goals, you itemise all of the components that are part of the end product. It is easy to run out of time if you underestimate what is involved in completing an assignment or learning a new concept by not making a careful evaluation of the demands of the task. Second, as you make your list you will naturally prioritise the items. What has to be done first and what can wait until later? Third, by writing down the items you make a more concrete commitment to getting the work done. It is almost as though you are writing a contract with yourself. You intend to complete the items from the list.

Initially, the major drawback of making lists is that you may underestimate the time required for completing tasks. With practice, though, it is possible to make the lists specific to your needs with reasonable and relevant items. For the list to be of maximum use it should be readily accessible and updated regularly. One warning though! Making lists does not get the work done. It is only the first step. A student may get sidetracked and spend hours of valuable time making lists and planning work, but never doing it, and that is not useful at all.

▷ **Flag Start Dates**

For big tasks, such as completing an essay or lab report or studying for an important test, you will need to plan very carefully. For example, if you have several exams in the final exam period, you may need to start your review several weeks in advance. When you have estimated how long the review will take, choose a starting date and record it on your calendar and also in your day book. If you plan your major tasks carefully and record starting dates well in advance, you will not find yourself running out of time or getting overwhelmed with major competing tasks.

▷ **Subdivide One Large Task into Many Smaller Tasks**

Seeing a task as a major undertaking can be very counter productive. A graduate student who was experiencing writer's block had at the top of her "*to do*" list, #1 -- *Write Thesis*. It was such an enormous undertaking that she had come to a complete standstill. Once she began to itemise manageable tasks for each week, she began to accomplish her larger goal. Being able to make small tasks out of one large one is an important component of effective time management. A mature student, who had a lot of home commitments in addition to his studying, had this down to a fine art! He was in the Honours English programme and had numerous essays each term. He allowed himself four weeks per essay. In week one he would gather his source materials together. In week two he read and researched his topic. In week three he wrote his essay, and in week four he revised his draft and produced the final copy. In any one week he might be working concurrently on several essays, all at different stages. He had the start dates for the different stages mapped out as soon as he received the assignment and knew the due dates -- what a great idea!

▷ **Plan Each Day**

Although all of your time management planning is important, it is the daily planning that is most closely linked to getting work done. Each evening you should think about the next day. How many classes do you have? What are the most pressing tasks? Do you have any non-academic commitments? How is your energy level and what do you think you can realistically accomplish tomorrow? Ideally, you should set goals of what you wish to accomplish, make decisions about where and when you are going to study, and locate any materials or other resources that you will need for the job.

If you have materials at hand and clear goals about what you wish to accomplish, you will find that it is easier to get started. You will not have to go through the step of asking yourself, "*What shall I do today*?" You will know where you have to begin.

▷ Engage in Time-Saving Tasks

If you want to be a very efficient learner and use your time well, you need to think carefully about ways of saving time. There are many such ways and you will need to evaluate what is appropriate to your own situation. There are two examples that are common to many students. For example, *always attend class* unless you have a very good reason for missing it. It always takes far longer to obtain and decipher notes from another student. You may miss key explanations or information about the course. Sometimes students will tell us that they can get the information just as readily from the textbooks, but these same students are often in trouble with their marks. Think through your decisions to miss classes very carefully.

An activity that can have a marked positive impact on memory, and can save a lot of future review time, is to *read through class notes within 24 hours* of taking them. Check that you fully understand the ideas, recorded the information clearly, and try to see how the details in the lecture relate to the theme or big picture. A little time spent in consolidation of ideas can save a lot of time in the long run.

▷ Be Flexible

Not all weeks in the school year will be equally busy. However well you plan, there will be some weeks when everything falls ready at the same time. You may have several assignments due and tests to write with very little time in between. On the other hand, there will be other weeks without such immediate pressure. Some of the most successful students are people who can be flexible. If the chips are down, and if it is one of those weeks when the pressure is on, they can respond positively and put in that extra push that is needed. Some people thrive on pressure while others fall apart. It is critical to know your limits and to manage your time within those limits. Flexibility of effort within reasonable limits is typical of an effective time manager.

Being flexible, however, does not mean leaving everything to the last minute, followed by "*all nighters*" to catch up on work to be done. The successful time manager is the student who plans flexibility into his or her schedule.

▷ Evaluate Your Progress

If you actively plan your time, evaluation of progress naturally follows. As you plan each day, you will evaluate whether or not you achieved the goals that you set for yourself. Monitoring your progress and accomplishments is an important component of effective time management. If you are not happy with how you are feeling, or with what you are accomplishing, you may need to rethink your initial goals.

WHAT'S YOUR CHOICE?

Many of the positive **time management principles** in this chapter will not be new to you. You may already be acting on many of them. However, it is also possible that you are not applying them as much as you would like. **What are your responses to the following twelve principles?**

	Is this principle one that is already part of my time management system?	Is this principle familiar to me but one that I rarely think about or apply?	Is this a new idea that I can build into my own time management system?	At what time in the school year would I need to think about, or apply, this principle?
Set Academic Goals				
Plan Ahead and Record Important Events				
Locate Useful Resources				
Find and Use a Good Work Location				
Know and Use your "Best Times"				
Make "To Do" Lists				
Flag Start Dates				
Subdivide One Large Task into Many Smaller Tasks				
Plan Each Day				
Engage in Time-Saving Tasks				
Be Flexible				
Evaluate your Progress				

CASE STUDY FOR REFLECTION

Review the positive time management principles introduced in this chapter and then advise Chris on how to deal with a difficult situation.

CHRIS: *"I'm having a really tough time this term. There have been a lot of problems at home and I'm finding it difficult to concentrate on my school work. Now I'm really behind and exams are only three weeks away! I'm hoping that you can give me some ideas so that I can do well on my exams. I don't want to lose my year. I just want to get through and hope that next year will be better. What would you suggest that I do?"*

_____

_____

_____

_____

_____

_____

_____

_____

_____

_____

_____

_____

_____

_____

## Chapter 4

YOUR ACTION PLAN

TOOLS FOR THE BASIC SYSTEM

- ▷ *Translating Principles into an Action Plan*
- ▷ *Goal Setting*
- ▷ *Recording Important Upcoming Events*
- ▷ *Flexible Planning*
- ▷ *Flag Start Dates*
- ▷ *An Ideal Work Location*
- ▷ *Your Resource List*
- ▷ *"Best Time" Tasks*
- ▷ *"To Do" Lists*
- ▷ *Daily Plans*
- ▷ *Time Savers*
- ▷ *Evaluation*

TROUBLE SHOOTING

QUESTIONS FOR REFLECTION

TOOLS FOR THE BASIC SYSTEM

▷ **Translating Principles into an Action Plan**

The questions and worksheets provided in this chapter are examples of organizers that you can use to translate the positive **time management principles** into your own **action plan**. They are the kinds of questions that you will ask and worksheets that you will use on a consistent basis, because the academic experience is very dynamic and decisions are made daily. In your action plan you will determine which organizers work best for you.

It is important to get a clear sense of the pattern of your regular academic and non-academic commitments in order to develop an effective schedule for studying outside class. If you manage your time efficiently, the times at which you study will fall into a pattern. For example, if you have a history class on Tuesday afternoon, you may read the assigned text on Monday evening so that you are well prepared for class. If you have a weekly math quiz on Friday mornings, you may review math problems on Thursdays. These are the most appropriate times to engage in these activities, resulting in maximum payoff from studying. **On the weekly schedule on the next page:**[1]

1. **Record all of the activities that happen in the same time slots each week.** In addition to classes, you will have regular non-academic activities such as clubs, sports, or a part-time job. Also record regular personal commitments, including meals, travel, and family time. Check that you have a reasonable balance of work and play, ensuring that you maintain a healthy attitude to your studies.

2. When all regularly occurring activities are recorded on the schedule, **select blocks of time for studying outside class.** For each day select two hours. You will likely need to add to these basic two hours but they will give you a regular, minimal base of study time. For each day of the week you will have two hours of regularly planned study time. This will reduce the number of decisions you need to make each day and will optimise your efficiency with time management.

3. When you have completed your basic weekly schedule, **assess whether or not your academic load is reasonable,** given your personal style of learning, your personal goals, and your non-academic commitments. Frustration can result from unrealistic expectations. If necessary you may have to make adjustments, either to the academic load or some of the lower priority non-academic activities.

---

[1] See Appendix B for additional worksheets

WEEKLY SCHEDULE

	Mon	Tues	Wed	Thur	Fri	Sat	Sun
7:00- 8:00							
8:00- 9:00							
9:00-10:00							
10:00-11:00							
11:00-12:00							
12:00- 1:00							
1:00- 2:00							
2:00- 3:00							
3:00- 4:00							
4:00- 5:00							
5:00- 6:00							
6:00- 7:00							
7:00- 8:00							
8:00- 9:00							
9:00-10:00							
10:00-11:00							

▷ **Goal Setting**

✓ *I want to run my own business some day*
✓ *I would like to get into the Social Work Programme*
✓ *I want to be well educated so that I can better understand modern problems*
✓ *I want to get this diploma so that I can get a better paying job*
✓ *I am developing my skill levels so that I can feel better about myself*

The goals that students have for their education are varied. Some goals relate to career opportunities and further education, as well as to personal growth and self esteem, and can have a very positive influence on motivation to do school work. On the other hand, if a student feels that it is not his or her own choice to be in school, or if a student has absolutely no career direction and does not enjoy academic work, then it is likely that this student will find it very difficult to complete necessary academic work. **What are your goals?**

1. Project ahead to a time **five years after you enter the workforce**. What kind of job are you doing and in what kind of setting? Also describe an acceptable alternative career goal.

_____

_____

_____

_____

2. Now think about **the present**. What are your academic goals for this current year?

_____

_____

3. Describe your **commitment** to the long-range and short-term goals that you have set for yourself.

_____

_____

▷ **Recording Important Upcoming Events**

Think carefully about each course that you are taking currently and, if there is a course outline, check it for important dates:

- *Are there scheduled readings to complete?*
- *When are the assigned tests or quizzes?*
- *Do you have to give class presentations?*
- *When are the essays or reports due?*

Also, are there personal or social events that you need to schedule into your school year? Special events such as family birthdays and weddings, holidays and religious days, sports events, and appointments with the dentist are just a few of the many activities for which you may have to plan.

Use a variety of organizers for recording important upcoming events:

1. *A Wall Calendar*

Make sure that the calendar has enough space for each day, so that you can clearly write on the calendar all necessary information. Also, hang the calendar in a location where you can check it frequently -- maybe above your desk.

2. *A Day-Planner*

A day-planner should be small enough to carry easily but large enough to contain all necessary information. An academic day-planner (beginning in July rather than January) is more convenient to use than a traditional diary. There are many versions of the academic day-planner on the market. Choose one carefully that fits your requirements. Prices vary greatly, from inexpensive to extremely expensive! Remember, it is not the cost of the day-planner that determines its usefulness; it is the way in which you use it. An inexpensive day-planner, put to good use, is just as effective as its more expensive counterparts.

Many schools now design day-planners specifically for their own students. These day-planners contain information on important school events, rules and regulations, and advertisements for useful resources. Check to see if such a day-planner is available from your school before you buy a commercial version.

3. *A Computer-Made Planner*

Many students now use computers as aids to learning. You may wish to design your own computer-made planners or use one of the many available commercial packages for time planning. On the following two pages, customise the planner bases for the next four months and record your important academic, personal and social upcoming events.

Sun	Mon	Tues	Wed	Thur	Fri	Sat

Sun	Mon	Tues	Wed	Thur	Fri	Sat

Sun	Mon	Tues	Wed	Thur	Fri	Sat

Sun	Mon	Tues	Wed	Thur	Fri	Sat

▷ Flexible Planning

The academic load will vary considerably from week to week throughout the academic term. In one week you may have a book report due as well as two term tests to write. You may be away from school on a job placement with hours of preparation each evening. In another week you may have no major commitments at all. Your personal and social life will also go through quiet and busy periods. For example, a student who participates in theatre productions will have many meetings and rehearsals to attend. An athlete will have to plan for practices and sports events. Recording upcoming events on a long-range planner makes it easier to pinpoint those busy weeks in the term for which extra planning is required.

Look back at the four-month planner that you have completed and **identify time periods when you can expect to be extra busy**. Think about how you will handle them. Flexibility is the key to surviving pressure and completing all of the necessary work. If you anticipate the extra-busy weeks and reduce as many non-essential activities as possible, you will be able to face the deadlines without being overwhelmed.

Try to be aware of your own limits for stress and increased workload. You may be motivated to put in long hours but find that you do not have the physical or mental stamina necessary. You may have a hard time staying awake or find that your thoughts are confused and your memory suddenly very poor. These are all signs of extreme tiredness and, however motivated the tired student might be, it is very difficult to do quality work when limits have been reached.

▷ Flag Start Dates

Running short of time is a very typical phenomenon for many students. Even though a student may have recorded due dates for major academic requirements, such as essays, presentations and tests, that same student may procrastinate about getting started on the necessary work. In part, this may be because the student misjudges the length of time needed for the task.

Look back again at the four-month planner and check the major academic requirements that you have recorded. For each, realistically estimate the amount of time that you will need, *within the context of the time you have available,* to complete the tasks involved. **Target your start date for each major academic requirement.** You will have to estimate how much time you will need for each. It is a good idea to set these flags for starting dates in a way that makes them stand out. You might colour them with a highlighter pen or use a different coloured pen or pencil to add the information.

▷ **An Ideal Work Location**

Finding a location, or locations, in which you can work well is very important to academic success. Imagine that you have a lot of work to complete. It is absolutely essential that you concentrate fully and work as efficiently as possible. Locate and describe, in as much detail as possible, the ideal setting for this concentrated study.

_____

_____

_____

_____

_____

▷ **Your Resource List**

Your day planner is the best place to record essential information, such as telephone numbers and locations of resources. People are probably your most useful resources. If your teachers are available outside class, then record times and locations where you can reach them. Also, record telephone numbers of friends and acquaintances from your various courses. Your peers can often help you with course problems and you may learn more from sharing information with each other than you would by studying completely alone. Also, schools, colleges and universities often provide a varied array of support services. For your own institution, check if the following resources are available and, if so, indicate if you know where they are located and how to use them:

☐ Library
☐ Course help centre
☐ Writing centre
☐ Learning skills services
☐ Counselling services
☐ Computers for student use
☐ Typing service
☐ Copy centre

☐ Student council office
☐ Recreational services
☐ Student awards office
☐ Off-campus services
☐ Residences services
☐ School newspaper
☐ School radio station
☐ Jobs centre

☐ Bookstore
☐ Computer store
☐ Health services
☐ Dental services
☐ Legal services
☐ Equity services
☐ Ombudsperson

▷ **"Best Time" Tasks**

Is your preferred style that of an *"early morning person,"* a *"daytimer,"* *"evenings only,"* a *"midnight owl,"* or a little bit of all four? Describe how the time of day affects your ability to do top quality work. Are there certain study tasks that best fit certain times of day for you? This information is necessary to making good decisions about the day-to-day study tasks that you plan.

_____

_____

_____

_____

_____

▷ **"To Do" Lists**

A very basic tool for students is the "to do" list. The items on the list are study tasks that need to be completed. If there is very little pressure and lots of time, this list may be carried around in a student's head. However, it is much more usual for students to have the combined pressure of many tasks at any point in time and, if these study tasks are not written down, they can be forgotten or postponed until it is too late to complete them adequately. This is particularly true of regular study tasks, such as reading the assigned pages of the text, solving math problems, or reviewing class notes soon after class. A manageable time frame for a "to do" list is a single week. Commonly, a successful student will plan on the weekend for the upcoming week.

The worksheet on the next page is an example of the type of list that can help you to plan each week. You can record three types of activities: course work tasks; personal events; and upcoming major tests and assignments, including dates. To be well prepared for making your own weekly "to do" list, first of all look back to the four-month planner and check for any major upcoming events. As you complete the following worksheet, try to limit the course work tasks so that you can complete a task in less than three hours. If a task will take longer than three hours, subdivide it into its constituent parts and record each part as a separate task on the list. **Subdividing major tasks into distinct manageable chunks** is an important principle of good time management.

"TO DO" LIST FOR WEEK OF _____

#	COURSE WORK TASKS	✓
1		
2		
3		
4		
5		
6		
7		
8		
9		
10		
12		

	PERSONAL	✓
1		
2		
3		
4		

UPCOMING MAJOR TESTS AND ASSIGNMENTS	DATE
1	
2	
3	

> **Daily Plans**

Although all aspects of time planning are important, it is the daily planning that is most critical because this is what gets the work done. It is best to plan ahead for the next day. Your weekly "to do" list is the guide for this decision making. Check your weekly list each evening and put a star beside the tasks with highest priority. These are your items for your daily plan. It takes practice to plan well. It is easy to be overly optimistic and to plan too much work for the time available. However, if you regularly set your daily goals, you will soon find the right load for you. When you decide what it is you wish to accomplish, make plans about when and where you will study. At the end of the day you can evaluate your progress and check the completed tasks off the list. This is a very satisfying activity!   Now, plan for tomorrow by completing the "Daily Plan Worksheet" below.

#	STUDY TASK	LOCATION AND TIME	✓
1			
2			
3			
4			

▷ **Time Savers**

One of the secrets of success as a student is getting work done efficiently. For example, Carlos may take one hour to develop a class plan for the kindergarten class while it takes Paul two hours to finish the same task. They both receive the same grade for their work, and so the extra time that Paul put into the task did not pay off in terms of marks. One of the misconceptions of students is that more time always means higher grades -- not necessarily so! A sample of suggestions for studying efficiently includes the following. For each, use the margin to reflect on your own experience. Are you happy with your performance or is there room for improvement?

Attend class

There are very obvious reasons for attending class. First, you will **HEAR** the information. This is a very powerful way to learn. As you listen to the teacher you encode important concepts in a different way than when you read about them. Second, it is a much faster method of gathering information. It will likely take you three times as long to gather the same quantity of information through reading the text. Third, you can ask questions of the teacher either during or at the end of the class. Also, there is often important extra information about tests and assignments presented in class. You can miss great clues if you do not attend.

Read through your class notes after class

This is possibly the most under used of the time-saving learning strategies. As you listen in class you absorb some, but not all, of the information. In class it is not easy to make all of the necessary connections or to understand ideas completely. You need time for reflection as you re-read your class notes soon after class, when the ideas are still fresh. It is rarely a good idea to rewrite your notes. Instead, it is better to consolidate the notes you have. As you re-read your notes respond to the following questions to improve the quality of your notes:

"Do I understand all of these ideas -- and if not -- where can I find information that will help?"

"Are my notes complete or do I need to add to them?"

"What do I need to do at this time to aid my memory of this information?"

Link individual facts to the big picture

If individual facts are not connected to a big picture, they are very difficult to remember and studying can take much more time and effort. First of all, make good use of any course outline that you have. See how the individual topics that are listed relate to the overall course objectives. Similarly, when you read from a text, first check the "Table of Contents" to see how the chapter that you are reading fits with its neighbours. Take particular note of headings and subheadings in class, and as you read the text, and relate incoming facts to their unifying themes. One student always asked the "so what" question when he had finished gathering information, that is,"*So what was that all about?*" The "so what" question, helps to keep the big picture clearly in mind.

Think, think, think

A very typical characteristic of successful students is that they really enjoy thinking! They think about course content many times a day, not only when sitting at a desk to study or listening in class. They think about ideas as they walk down the street, wash dishes, walk the dog or drive the car. If they have a major essay to write, they think about it long before putting pen to paper. When they begin the essay in earnest, they already have generated a selection of seminal ideas and the whole process proceeds more quickly. Also, memory is very much enhanced by regular reflection about course topics. The exercise of retrieving information from memory, and associating ideas conceptually, strengthens the memory traces and ensures that future retrieval of that same information is facilitated. A sound memory can save a lot of review time for tests.

Place time limits on tasks

As far as possible, place reasonable time limits on academic tasks. For example, go to the library with a clear goal in mind -- "*I will use this one afternoon to find suitable materials for my essay.*" Also, when you have an assigned reading to complete, set a reasonable goal for how long the reading should take. You can have considerable control over time if this is a priority issue for you and you set the limits. You will need to develop a sound sense of the time requirements for tasks.

▷ **Evaluation**

For most students there are two clear measures of whether or not their time management strategies are working well: grades and energy level. If your grades are unsatisfactory, or if your grades are satisfactory but you are feeling tired and overwhelmed by the pressure of school work, then time management may be part of the problem. However, remember that, although time management strategies contribute both to academic success and to feelings of well being, there may be other reasons why grades or energy levels are low. A teacher or a counsellor at your school may be able to help you with problems.

If there is a problem, evaluate the decisions that you make about time. For example, keep a **time log** by recording your daily activities in a small notebook or on your computer. Add comments about your time use. One student noted, "*I am amazed to find that travel time today was over 90 minutes! I live in residence on campus and am in the habit of going from and to the dorm for my classes. Now I plan to work in the central library in between classes.*" **What do you think are the main time management problems indicated in the daily log recorded by Brandon?**

Tuesday: Got up at 7.30 as planned and made it to the 8.30 class. After class went to the cafeteria with Mo -- joined by Mitch and Deidre. Didn't get to library until 11.00. Found journals I needed and read from 11.20 - 1.00. Class from 1-3. Didn't get down to work again 'till 9.00, (met Leila, travel time, laundry, eats, TV!) Read Biology and finished French exercises. Tired by 11.00 so watched TV for two hours before bed.

TROUBLE SHOOTING

Use the space below to write your time log for **yesterday**. Evaluate your use of time and look for anything that you could have done differently. In particular, track for bad habits that you recognise and on which you wish to work.

_____

_____

_____

_____

_____

_____

_____

_____

_____

QUESTIONS FOR REFLECTION

- *What organizers do you currently use for managing time?*
- *Given your class schedule, when are the best "out of class" study times for you?*
- *What effects do your goals have on the way that you manage your time?*
- *What kind of problems do you experience as you manage your time around major events?*
- *Describe your typical reaction to extra-busy weeks in the school term.*
- *What resources do you find are the most useful for your academic programme?*
- *Describe any of your own "time-saving" academic strategies.*
- *How do you evaluate whether or not your time management strategies are working?*

## Chapter 5

MOTIVATION AND CONCENTRATION

BEING YOUR ACADEMIC BEST

- ▷ *The Daily Demands of Student Life*
- ▷ *Energy + Enthusiasm = Motivation*

KNOW YOUR TYPE

- ▷ *Common Patterns*
  - *The Perfectionist*
  - *The "On the Spur of the Moment" Decision Maker*
  - *The Game Player*
  - *The "Count me in" Student Type*
  - *The "I'll be at the Library" Student Type*
- ▷ *The Successful Time Manager*

CONCENTRATION

- ▷ *A Sense of Commitment*
- ▷ *Dealing with Distractions*

QUESTIONS FOR REFLECTION

BEING YOUR ACADEMIC BEST

▷ The Daily Demands of Student Life

Imagine the following scene. The alarm rings on a cold, rainy school morning. There is no one to tell you to go to school and the bed feels so comfortable. Do you get up and go to class or do you roll over and go back to sleep? This is a typical dilemma that challenges students every school year. While most students share the desire to succeed at school, when given the choice some students turn off the alarm and go back to sleep. These same students may even proclaim that they are deeply committed to their education, but actions speak louder than words.

The motivation to tackle the daily demands of student life is an essential ingredient of good time management and academic success. Students need to be motivated to attend classes, keep up with course readings, study in advance of tests, and work diligently on essays and assignments. If this sounds too much like hard work to you, an evaluation of your reasons for being in school is probably a good idea. Sometimes students are swayed by the saying, *"School days are the best days of your life."* Their primary motivation is to socialise at the expense of academic achievement, with the end result being disappointing "school days".

There *is* some truth in this expression. School days can be the best days of your life, especially in terms of intellectual growth. They are a time for you to exercise your brain by developing thinking skills and acquiring knowledge that likely will serve you well in the future, both personally and professionally. With good time management there can also be room for fun and relaxation. When good friends and fun times are combined with academic success, this truly can be a wonderful time in your life.

An over emphasis on fun is not the only reason for feeling unmotivated to meet the daily demands of student life. Sometimes motivation is a problem because students do not perceive courses or programmes as being relevant to their personal goals. Also, it is hard to get actively involved in school if interest is lacking or if the primary reason for being in a programme is to please someone else.

Problems with motivation can also surface if students feel frustrated or overwhelmed. Consider the motivation level of the student who fails a test and is thinking, *"It's going to be difficult to do well in this course now, so why bother?"* It may feel easier to give up than to rise to the challenge. Other factors that can diminish motivation include personal problems, attempting to tackle too much within the available time, being overly critical of oneself, and even lack of sleep.

▷ **Energy + Enthusiasm = Motivation**

Motivation is crucial to effective time management and academic success. Think of something that you learned well in the past and can still recall with seemingly little effort. Perhaps you can think of the words of a song or the statistics of a favourite sports team. Motivation to learn these pieces of information arose naturally because you had the energy and enthusiasm to acquire new knowledge. Energy and enthusiasm are key components of motivation. In order to capture these you may have to make some decisions based on an assessment of your situation. Consider the following questions:

- *Do you place school commitments before socialising?*
- *Does your present academic programme correspond with your long-term goals?*
- *Are you genuinely interested in your courses?*
- *Do you persevere despite academic setbacks?*
- *Are you able to keep personal issues from interfering with school?*
- *Are your present expectations realistic given the demands on your time?*
- *Are you supportive in what you say to yourself?*
- *Do you get adequate sleep and nutrition?*

If you answered *"no"* to any of these questions, your academic effectiveness is probably being hurt by difficulties with motivation. **What decisions can you make to strengthen your motivation?** One option is to change your approach to school. For example, you can generate interest in a course by speaking with the instructor or you can improve effectiveness by meeting with a counsellor to discuss learning strategies. You can also remind yourself that, while school years can be a time for meeting new people, your number one priority is your education. This means ensuring that there is a reasonable time allotted for school and that sleep is not being compromised.

If nothing seems to improves your motivation level you may have to make decisions about your situation, such as changing your programme, reducing your course load, or even leaving school. Only you can assess if you should focus on changing your approach to school or whether it is desirable or possible to change your situation. **What suggestions would you offer to the following students?**

Jordan's heart just isn't into school. *He feels as though he's just going through the motions - getting up, going to class, coming home. Even though his marks are well below the class average, he doesn't care. His motivation is at an all-time low. He knows what the problem is: he doesn't want to be a lawyer. But it seems to mean so much to his parents; they're already talking about, "Our son, the lawyer." Besides, he hasn't given much thought to any alternatives - except for journalism. Reporting on current events interests him.*

Margaret feels like a juggler just before the pins come tumbling down. *A lot has happened in the ten years since she's last been in school, including marriage, children, and divorce. Before classes started she was confident that she was working towards a better future and she enthusiastically embraced academic life by taking a full course load. Now she isn't so sure. Her marks are mediocre, she's struggling financially after cutting back on hours at her part-time job, and she's exhausted and irritable during the little time that she has with her children. She is increasingly concerned that the sacrifices will not be worth the effort, and she's considering quitting school.*

As you can see from Jordan and Margaret's experiences, there are no easy answers. However, by identifying problems with motivation and assessing individual circumstances, students are better equipped to make important decisions. It is essential for students to motivate themselves, but is this best accomplished by adapting the approach to studying or by changing the situation? The answer lies in thinking about underlying causes and possible solutions to motivation problems. The following *Motivation Action Plan* offers some suggestions for Jordan and Margaret, and provides space for you to identify a motivation problem of your own, explore the underlying causes, and propose possible solutions.

MOTIVATION ACTION PLAN		
Motivation Problem	*Underlying Causes*	*Possible Solutions*
<u>JORDAN</u> • rarely feels like studying • doesn't have good learning skills, eg. procrastinates/poor time management; unprepared for tests • unconcerned about below average grades	• dislikes program - doesn't see it as a personal goal; doing it only for his parents • bored with courses - lacks genuine interest • doing poorly may force a decision: by failing he may be able to pursue personal goals (*if his low marks don't block his options!*)	✓ explore alternatives - consider implications of changing programmes (*i.e., worth costs in terms of time and money?*) or leaving school (*i.e., impact on employment opportunities?*) ✓ continue with programme and work to generate interest (*i.e., talk to enthusiastic peers & teachers, remind self of benefits of completing programme - good background for journalism*)
<u>MARGARET</u> • never seems to find sufficient time for school work • exhausted all of the time - lack of quality time with children • highly anxious -- worried about failing after investing so much time and money	• juggling too much at once - school, work, family, etc. • pace of schedule allows for no relaxation time • if low marks persist, may not be accepted into programme of choice & pursue career goal -- uncertainty re: future	✓ realistically assess demands on time. An option to withdrawing from school is reducing course load (*this may mean taking longer to reach goal, but higher grades & quality time with children*) ✓ meet with learning skills counsellor re: managing anxiety & suggestions to improve marks

KNOW YOUR TYPE

▷ Common Patterns

While lack of motivation can result for a number of reasons, including lack of interest, frustration over low marks, and worry, it may also reflect an habitual approach to school on the part of a student. There are a number of common patterns of behaviour that can cause motivation problems if carried to extremes. **While it is unusual to fit neatly into only one pattern, can you see elements of your approach in any of the following behaviour types?**

• The Perfectionist

The perfectionist is motivated to do an exceptional job on every academic task. This type of student works very hard and tries to complete all of the assigned work without any short cuts at all. While conscientiousness and diligence can be strengths, perfectionism becomes a weakness when a student is not very strategic or cue aware. The student is inefficient because he or she believes that everything is equally important and requires a lot of work. It is important to prioritise tasks and make time-saving decisions, especially during busy times of the school year.

• The "On the Spur of the Moment" Decision Maker

The "on the spur of the moment" decision maker usually does not plan ahead. Although the student may be motivated to do school work, it is always a last minute rush. This in itself may not be a problem. Indeed, a strength for some students is working under the pressure of an imminent deadline. Weaknesses with this behaviour pattern become apparent, however, if competing tasks combine to create an unmanageable load. Without the benefit of foresight, the student may be forced to submit substandard work or sacrifice studying in order to complete assignments.

• The Game Player

This type of student is very strategic and cue aware - often to an extreme degree. The game player is motivated by the desire to do the minimum amount of work for the maximum pay off. This approach can prove to be a significant strength. The student prioritises tasks, makes good use of resources, such as talking to instructors and accessing old exams, and listens intently for cues as to what content is especially important. The negative element to the game player is evident in the student who constantly manipulates the system to get deadlines extended. This can backfire if extensions compound or if the student gets a reputation for lateness.

• The "Count me in" Student Type

This is the student who is motivated to be involved in a lot more than academic course work. Extracurricular involvement may include political activities, such as being a member of student council, sports, paid employment, volunteer work, and social activities. While personal development certainly can be enhanced by varied pursuits, particular attention must be paid to prioritising among competing endeavours. With a wide range of interests and only 24 hours in the day, the "count me in" student needs strong time management skills. When poor time management collides with active involvement in a variety of activities, the end result is often incomplete assignments and below-potential performance.

• The "I'll be at the Library" Student Type

The "I'll be at the library" student has limited involvement in activities outside school. For this type of student, academic activities absorb significant amounts of available time. There are different reasons why a student may be motivated to focus almost exclusively on school, including genuine intellectual fervour or fear that anything less than 100% dedication will result in failure. The advantages and disadvantages of this approach are linked closely to the personality characteristics of the student; some students manage splendidly while others cope very poorly when school work becomes the major component of their lives. It is this distinction that helps to determine whether the behaviour pattern is problematic or not.

Which behaviour type do you identify with most closely?

_____

_____

What are the strengths and weaknesses of this approach for you?

_____

_____

_____

_____

▷ **The Successful Time Manager**

Successful time managers are not born, but evolve with experience. These are students who maintain both physical and emotional health and are often able to achieve academic goals by having a balance of activities in their school and extra-curricular experiences. They may have elements of the perfectionist, the "on the spur of the moment" decision maker, the game player, the "count me in" or the "I'll be in the library" student types. Effective time managers maximize the strengths and minimize the weaknesses of behaviour patterns. They also appreciate the need to motivate themselves.

Self motivation can take many forms. One student wrote a pep talk in each of his textbooks early in the school year when he was optimistic and enthusiastic. In the front of each book he noted, (1) why he was taking the course, (2) what he could find inherently interesting in the course, and (3) he listed how it contributed to his short-term and long-term plans. When asked why he did this he answered, *"I know that there will come a time in the school year when I just don't feel like opening the textbook. When this happens, I open the cover, read my ready-made pep talk, and it's enough to get me back to work."* This student was keenly aware of the important role that motivation plays in academic success. And who knows, maybe the inscribed pep talks even help the resale!

CONCENTRATION

Motivation is not the only ingredient for successful time management. Once motivation to put forth a good effort is in place, the ability to focus on the task at hand is crucial. Just as students can increase their level of motivation, they can enhance concentration to improve overall effectiveness.

▷ **A Sense of Commitment**

Concentration can be enhanced by generating interest and enthusiasm. Have you ever been so absorbed in something that you were surprised when you discovered the amount of time that had elapsed? This demonstrates a high level of concentration. Students who capture a sense of commitment for their studies increase the likelihood that concentration (and academic success) will follow. If you intend to continue with a course or programme, it is in your best interest to convince yourself that the associated study tasks are interesting and worth the effort. Without a sense of commitment, it is easy to become apathetic. When this occurs, both motivation and concentration suffer.

▷ **Dealing with Distractions**

Even when students are committed to achieving academic goals, sometimes attention is divided between a task and competing distractions. By being aware of these distractions, a student can take positive steps to minimize their degree of interference. Think about the following strategies for dealing with both internal and external distractions.

Examples of INTERNAL Distractions	• difficulty studying (because hungry, sleepy, too hot, or too cold)	• *problem concentrating (because keep thinking of personal issues)*	• lose interest as time elapses (just trying to get task done regardless of quality)
Suggestions to strengthen concentration	✓ consider time of day and location when planning study time ✓ plan for meals and rest ✓ find a good place to work	✓ *practice thought stopping* ✓ *redirect attention back to task* ✓ *plan time to deal with ongoing distracting thoughts*	✓ use small chunks of time ✓ assess attention every 30 minutes ✓ self test to help focus and ensure absorbing information

Examples of EXTERNAL Distractions	• *difficulty studying (because setting too noisy)*	• watching activities of others (distracted by things in vicinity)	• *lose focus after reading a few pages (experience eye strain)*
Suggestions to strengthen concentration	✓ *plan study environment that is conducive to getting work done* ✓ *determine what noise level suits you and seek a corresponding work setting* ✓ *go to library*	✓ locate desk so it is not overlooking activity (ie. face blank wall) ✓ clear desk of excess materials ✓ make others aware of study times to minimize interruptions	✓ *consider type of lighting - is room adequately lit?* ✓ *deflect desk lamp off wall to avoid glare* ✓ *make appointment to have eyes checked*

QUESTIONS FOR REFLECTION

- *What are some general reasons for lack of motivation to tackle academic tasks?*

- *Discuss the roles of energy and enthusiasm in maintaining a high level of motivation.*

- *Is your academic effectiveness being hindered by problems with motivation? If yes, what decisions can you make to strengthen motivation?*

- *If motivation is a problem for you, what are some changes to your approach to your studies or to your situation that you can make?*

- *Which behaviour pattern most closely depicts your motivation type?*

- *Does your academic performance benefit from your approach to school or suffer because of it?*

- *How can you motivate yourself?*

- *Are you able to concentrate well when tackling school work?*

- *How can you improve your concentration skills?*

Chapter 6

BEATING THE PROCRASTINATION HABIT

THE PROCRASTINATION BLUES

> ▷ *Rising to the Student Challenge*
> ▷ *The Cost of Procrastinating*

THE SYMPTOMS

> ▷ *Identifying Procrastinating Behaviour*

UNDERSTANDING THE PROBLEM

> ▷ *Fear of Failure*
> ▷ *Fear of Success*
> ▷ *The Perfectionist*
> ▷ *The Rebel*
> ▷ *Being Overwhelmed*
> ▷ *Lack of Interest*
> ▷ *An Established Pattern*

SOLVING THE PROBLEM

> ▷ *Identify the Roadblocks*
> ▷ *Develop an Action Plan*
> ▷ *The Importance of Rewards*

QUESTIONS FOR REFLECTION

THE PROCRASTINATION BLUES

▷ Rising to the Student Challenge

Who has not experienced the procrastination blues? You know the feeling --
you *really* do not feel like working, but there are *so many* reminders of things that
need to get done. Torn, you may find that very little is accomplished when you try
to work, and feelings of guilt and worry set in when you do not work.

As a group, students may be particularly vulnerable to procrastinating. No
supervisor oversees productivity and no pay cheque offers a reward for the effort put
forth. The rewards of student effort are often intangible, such as new insights and
intellectual growth. Other rewards are long term. For example, graduating from
school may lead to increased employment opportunities or a fulfilling career. With
rewards that are not immediate, there may be an increased tendency to procrastinate.

▷ The Cost of Procrastinating

Most people procrastinate from time to time, but chronic procrastination can
undermine the effectiveness of a student. **What are some costs of procrastinating?**

> ✓ *submitting work that reflects cramming*
> ✓ *not submitting work and facing the consequences*
> ✓ *increased stress levels*
> ✓ *increased likelihood of a poor academic performance resulting in
>   reduced education and career options*

Why sabotage effectiveness through procrastination? This predicament *can*
be avoided by (1) being aware of the symptoms, (2) understanding the problem, and
(3) implementing strategies to beat the procrastination habit.

THE SYMPTOMS

▷ Identifying Procrastinating Behaviour

Students can procrastinate in some amazingly creative ways. Entire apartments can be redecorated in the days leading up to a test. Sometimes great lengths are taken by a student to appear to be *not* procrastinating. Hours can be spent colour coding work schedules and timetables. One student even procrastinated by enroling in a procrastination workshop three times in one academic year!

Awareness of procrastination may not be enough to change this pattern. A student, recognizing her tendency to be distracted at home, wisely decided to work in the library. She found a quiet location and took out her textbooks -- then she went floor to floor searching for someone she knew. She intended to work in the library, but once in the library she spent her time socializing. Procrastination, the time robber, had struck.

The obvious symptom of procrastination is that the student does not begin the required task. However, there is a diverse range of behaviours that may also reflect procrastination. Consider the situations confronting the following students. **Can you identify with any of them?**

Pat is puzzled. *With two papers and a test in the upcoming week, he finds himself absorbed by a variety of tasks: cleaning the house, doing the laundry, and even organizing his books in alphabetical order! Every time he intends to get down to work, he finds something else to do. He knows that if he doesn't focus on his school work soon he'll be in trouble, but he just can't seem to break the pattern that's been established.*

Amanda is amazing. *Even though she's carrying a full load of courses, she's always the first to volunteer to help friends and to work extra shifts at her part-time job. She's also rehearsing evenings for a school play! How does she do it? Well, she has four overdue essays, she crams all night for tests, and she may be forced to drop a course or two.*

> **Sam is sleepy.** *Usually full of energy, it seems that whenever he picks up a textbook he is overcome with fatigue. Yawning, he is convinced that after a short nap he'll be able to concentrate. The problem is, he's spending a lot of time sleeping and very little time on assignments.*

While involved in very different activities, Puzzled Pat, Amazing Amanda and Sleepy Sam are all procrastinating. Behaviours that may reflect procrastination include spending a lot of time on low priority tasks, seeking out company all of the time, volunteering to help a variety of good causes, and sleeping a lot. **What behaviours are symptoms of procrastination for you?**

UNDERSTANDING THE PROBLEM

The underlying reasons for procrastinating may differ considerably from student to student. If you are a procrastinator and wish to beat the procrastination habit, consider why you engage in this self-defeating pattern. **Do you recognize yourself in any of the following examples?**

▷ **Fear of Failure**

When it comes to school, Valerie isn't very confident. She worries that she's not smart enough to succeed. To avoid having this fear realized, she provides herself with excuses by procrastinating.

In the case of fear of failure, the student may have received some negative feedback in the past or be feeling overwhelmed by a particular course or programme. It feels safer to avoid real evaluation of performance by procrastinating and either avoiding the assignment altogether, or to have the excuse of a "rushed" job. Procrastination may be used as a way of controlling disappointment. Some students set low goals to protect themselves from really trying and being disappointed if they should fail, but by procrastinating there is an increased likelihood of failure.

▷ **Fear of Success**

Initially, Brian was pleasantly surprised by his success in school. Soon, however, his progress slowed to the point where he isn't keeping up with his readings and is missing classes. Brian observes that his best friend - who chose a job over school - seems depressed and irritable whenever Brian talks about school. Success might mean hurting and losing his friend, so Brian is hurting himself by becoming a procrastinator.

In the example of fear of success, a really good performance sets up expectations from others about the student's overall potential. This can be threatening for many reasons, including that success may threaten those closest to the student, such as a spouse or a close peer. Procrastination is a way of ensuring a poor academic performance rather than risk losing an important relationship. Another option, however, is an open discussion to attempt to resolve the conflict.

Fear of success can also contribute to procrastination if a student does not want top marks. After all, once a high standard is established, there will be the continued pressure of having to maintain it. For some students that seems like a lot of hard work. In both cases, however, the student is sacrificing opportunity.

▷ The Perfectionist

Michelle's high standards demand an outstanding academic performance. Being a successful student means everything to her, but lately she can't seem to finish important tasks. She over researches essays and leaves too little time to write a "brilliant" paper.

The perfectionist has the unrealistic expectation that an outstanding job must be performed for every task. As a result, it may not be until it is too late to put forth an exceptional effort that assignments get finished. Instead of redefining what constitutes doing a good job - conscientiously tackling a task while appreciating both deadlines and the importance of other demands - the perfectionist procrastinates because any effort is deemed never quite good enough. When standards are set too high, incomplete or late assignments are not uncommon.

▷ The Rebel

Adam wonders who this teacher thinks she is -- telling him what to do. It's bad enough that the only reason why he's taking this course is to satisfy his folks. He resents the pressure and the expectations. He'll do the work all right, but on his own terms.

Some people react very negatively to the idea of imposed deadlines. It is as though control is taken away from the individual and imposed by a higher authority. For students who have had negative past experiences - often outside the academic setting - this attitude can create a barrier to their successful completion of tasks.

It is important for the student to assess who is being hurt the most by rebelling through procrastination. Very likely, it is the student. Perhaps with a less rebellious and more positive attitude, genuine interest can be stimulated or alternative academic and career goals can be explored.

▷ Being Overwhelmed

With the term progressing, Jennifer feels as though she is drowning. She's behind in her readings, has two papers due, and needs to prepare for an upcoming test. "It's impossible to complete all of this," she thinks. The more she thinks about all the work she has to do, the less she gets done and the further behind she becomes.

For some students, procrastination sets in when workloads become too heavy. Feeling overwhelmed, there is a tendency for some students to throw their arms up in despair and not tackle anything, rather than to sit down and make some important judgment calls about where to begin to work.

During crunch times, it is especially crucial to be strategic. Decisions need to be made about what to concentrate on. It is important to remember that any work completed is progress and will contribute to overall effectiveness.

▷ Lack of Interest

"Boring" is the word that Michael uses most often to describe school. He can't remember when he last felt interested in class and is questioning whether or not he wants to continue with school. He wonders what's the point of working if he isn't going to continue. Maybe if he just keeps procrastinating the decision to quit will be made for him.

A student can lose interest in school for many reasons. Perhaps the course content does not capture the attention of the student, or personal issues interfere with concentration. The student may lose momentum and lack the energy to stay involved, perhaps because of poor sleeping or eating habits.

As a student, there is a responsibility to approach school conscientiously. It is the student's responsibility to attend classes, get adequate sleep, and generate interest in courses. If these seem impossible, perhaps the student is well advised to consider the role that school plays in her or his life, and to explore alternatives. If distracting personal issues persist, a realistic appraisal of priorities may assist in determining whether academic goals need to be delayed or courseloads lightened.

▷ An Established Pattern

For as long as Catherine can remember she has always been able to get good marks with last minute effort. Convinced that she works best under pressure, she waits until the last possible moment to start assignments or study for tests...and it works -- until now. With a large volume of reading to get through, and exams that test applications not just memory, she is really struggling. Still, maybe on the next test she'll find that the "old system" still works (...but it probably won't).

It is not uncommon for students to leave projects until the last minute and then to pull "all nighters" to get them completed. This pattern becomes part of the student's repertoire of study approaches and may, for a while, be successful. However, there is a tendency for such a pattern to become a problem, especially as the academic demands of programmes increase. If academic success is to be attained, it may be time to break the procrastination habit.

SOLVING THE PROBLEM

In reviewing some symptoms of procrastination and attempting to understand the problem, the complexity of this issue becomes apparent. Indeed, the underlying reasons for procrastinating may vary from course to course and a student may exhibit different symptoms at different times. The important thing is that the student really wants to beat the procrastination habit.

How does a student start to break the procrastination habit and become an effective time manager? There are two main steps to take to begin solving the problem of procrastination:

> ▷ **identify the roadblocks**
> ▷ **develop an action plan**

Keeping in mind that change often occurs one step at a time, complete the following exercises. By investing some time and thought on this problem now, you are contributing to a less stressful and more rewarding future.

▷ **Identify the Roadblocks**

The purpose of this exercise is to increase your awareness of personal symptoms of procrastination and to highlight how these symptoms are linked to your thoughts and feelings. It is also intended to encourage you to consider the reasons underlying this type of behaviour. By (1) identifying the roadblocks posed by your time wasters, (2) examining your rationale for procrastinating, and (3) exploring accompanying feelings, you will have taken a step towards positive change.

Imagine that you have an essay to hand in for a political science class. Describe yourself on the last day before the assignment is due, but it has yet to be started. Use the following questions to guide your descriptions.

How have you wasted time this past week?

_____

_____

_____

What are you doing on the last day before the assignment is due?

_____

_____

_____

What are you saying to yourself?

_____

_____

_____

How are you feeling?

_____

_____

_____

You have taken a step towards solving the problem of procrastination by answering these questions. You have identified some roadblocks, and in doing so, increased your awareness of your personal procrastination issues. You can go a step further by summarising the main points.

When you procrastinate, what are your symptoms?

What do your self talk, feelings, and insights suggest about your underlying reasons for procrastinating?

▷ **Develop an Action Plan**

Simply recognising *how* and *why* procrastination occurs does not bring about change. A plan of action is needed to deal with procrastination. While action plans can take a variety of forms, they share a common goal: to increase overall effectiveness. For example, you can develop an action plan to deal with the time wasters that you have identified. First, take a look at the completed example and then use the worksheet on the next page to implement a plan of your own.

Example 1: An action plan to deal with time wasters
✓ identify time wasters
✓ specify realistic solutions
✓ implement solutions
✓ monitor progress

★ Time waster	#1 Spending evenings talking with roommate rather than doing work	#2 Constantly interrupted by others in the house	#3 Getting hooked on a TV show and then watching TV all evening
Realistic solutions	• *go to the library!* • *use day-time hours between classes for school work* • *during week socialize only between 10-11 p.m.*	• *close my bedroom door while working* • *tell housemates that I wish to be undisturbed for two hours* • *be firm about interruptions*	• *plan ahead which shows I want to watch and use them as rewards for work accomplished* • *resist casual TV watching!* • *work away from the TV*
Implement Solutions			
Check-in 1 week	• *using time between classes better* • *need to talk to roommate re:interruptions*	• *my plan working with three out of four housemates* • *talk with Les about interruptions*	• *not watching as much TV* • *feel good about more control over TV watching*
Check-in 1 month	• *Yes! It's working (and so am I!!)*	• *all of us are getting more work done!* • *still a bit of a cool atmosphere with Les but that's okay*	• *look forward each week to planned TV viewing* • *getting more work done* • *marks have improved!*

Your personal action plan to deal with time wasters

✓ *identify time wasters*
✓ *specify realistic solutions*
✓ *implement solutions*
✓ *monitor progress*

★ Time waster	#1	#2	#3
Realistic solutions			
Implement Solutions			
Check-in 1 week			
Check-in 1 month			

Another type of action plan can be devised to help tackle major assignments. By dividing large assignments into smaller tasks they become more manageable, which decreases the probability of procrastinating and increases the quality of the work submitted. Consider the following inventory of reasonable goals that a student might set for completion of a major assignment. On a separate piece of paper, develop your own action plan for an upcoming assignment.

Example 2: An action plan to deal with major assignments
✓ *identify a major assignment*
✓ *list specific tasks that will contribute to its completion*
✓ *organize tasks into realistic actions with time frames*
✓ *incorporate actions into weekly plan*

ASSIGNMENT: 2,500 word research essay due in six weeks		
Week	**Task**	**Action**
1	• **Go to library** *(approx. 1-3 hours)* • **Check-in with instructor** *(approx. 5-30 minutes)*	▸ conduct preliminary research to assess availability of information and define and narrow focus of topic. *(Reminder! Beware of gathering large amounts of information that may prove to be irrelevant; work on providing a focus for future research)* ▸ clarify any questions regarding the assignment and verify that focus is 'on track'
2	• **Go to library** *(approx. 2-4 hours)* • **Develop working thesis/outline** *(approx. 1-2 hours)*	▸ gather research materials using focus to guide search ▸ identify the main focus of the essay and determine how paper will proceed *(Note! Save time by clearly outlining components of essay)*
3	• **Read/organize research** *(approx. 6-20 hours)*	▸ read selectively with clear focus, identifying relevant information and organizing key points within outline
4	• **Rough draft(s)** *(approx. 6-20 hours)*	▸ start writing: build on outline, incorporate research. *(Caution! Don't spend too much time researching & too little time writing)*
5	• **Final draft** *(approx. 4-10 hours)*	▸ polish and proofread essay, check for grammar, spelling, transition sentences, etc. *(Hint! Read aloud to assess flow of paper)*
6	• **Submit quality assignment on time**	▸ congratulations on a job well done! It's time for a well-deserved reward.

▷ **The Importance of Rewards**

Identifying roadblocks and developing action plans are important steps in solving the problem of procrastination. Even with good intentions, however, old patterns may resurface. Students can become discouraged and have a sense that change is impossible. Habits do not tend to change over night, so patience and persistence are called for. You can help to foster change, however, by incorporating rewards into your action plan.

Sometimes students try to beat the procrastination habit by punishing themselves. They may deny themselves breaks, or contribute to feelings of guilt by continually comparing themselves to friends who are high achievers or by berating themselves. Given these negative associations with change, it is not surprising that the procrastination habit resurfaces.

There *is* an alternative to this negative approach to changing behaviour. Research evidence supports the position that it is more effective to encourage change through rewards, than to force change through punishment. Take some time to explore both small and large rewards as part of your action plan to become a better time manager, and plan to implement these self motivators.

Rewards vary from individual to individual. What is considered by one student to be a reward, may not necessarily be viewed as such by another student. Carefully consider what constitutes rewards for you.

Examples of small rewards may include:
- *spending an hour every day listening to music or watching TV*
- *designating Friday evenings as social time*
- *allotting regular time each week for hobbies or interests*
- *spending time on a favourite course after working on a less enjoyable course*

Examples of large rewards may include:
- *planning for a vacation during the winter or summer break*
- *making good use of time during the week so that Sunday can be a family day*
- *the increased opportunities that an education will provide over your lifetime*
- *guilt free, peace of mind knowing that, through planning, relaxation time is not taking away from your studies, but enhancing them*

Realistic small rewards that you will make part of your action plan are:

_____

_____

_____

_____

Realistic large rewards that you will make part of your action plan are:

_____

_____

_____

_____

QUESTIONS FOR REFLECTION

- *What time management challenges are unique to your situation?*
- *What are some of the costs of procrastinating?*
- *List some possible symptoms of procrastinating behaviour. How do you procrastinate?*
- *When you procrastinate, do you understand why? If yes, elaborate.*
- *What are some roadblocks that you must overcome in order to beat the procrastination habit?*
- *Describe an action plan that can contribute to your effectiveness and productivity.*
- *What rewards will assist you in positive change?*

## Chapter 7

EXPERIENCING STRESS

WHAT IS STRESS?

    ▷ *Positive and Negative Stress*
    ▷ *Individual Responses to Stress*

RECOGNISING SYMPTOMS OF STRESS

    ▷ *Physical*
    ▷ *Emotional*
    ▷ *Behavioural*
    ▷ *Cognitive*

MANAGING DISTRESS

    ▷ *Deep Breathing Techniques*
    ▷ *Muscle Relaxation*
    ▷ *Exercise*
    ▷ *Self Talk*
    ▷ *Visual Imagery*
    ▷ *Sharing with Others*

A HEALTHY LIFESTYLE

    ▷ *Maintaining Stress Busters*

QUESTIONS FOR REFLECTION

WHAT IS STRESS?

Stress is a normal and inevitable part of life. Virtually any change that we experience causes stress. Exercising, going on vacation, and even getting up in the morning are all examples of stressors that require us to respond in some way. Student life is full of stressors. These include writing exams, presenting seminars, doing assignments and attending classes. Other stressors may include changing schools, deciding on a career, and balancing academic expectations with family, work, and social demands. In itself, stress is neither good nor bad. How we respond to stress, however, determines whether it has a positive or negative effect on our lives.

▷ Positive and Negative Stress

While many people tend to think of stress in negative terms, stress can be viewed as a positive force in our lives. How many times have you heard someone say, *"Once the pressure was on, I was really able to get a lot of work done"*? Positive stress acts as a motivating force in our lives. For some people, it enables them to tap into the strength needed to climb mountains and run marathons. For students, stress can gear you up for exams and help focus concentration on the task at hand. This occurs because stress results in a surge of energy as the body produces adrenalin. Positive stress occurs if this energy is used to tackle a challenge; afterwards, we are able to relax. Positive stress is nature's way of providing us with the energy and concentration to accomplish an endeavour, whether it be academic, athletic, or personal.

But what happens when this surge of adrenalin is not used to tackle the task at hand, or when we do not relax afterwards? Negative stress, also referred to as distress, occurs. Consider the student who faces the challenge of two tests and a major assignment in the upcoming week. This stressful situation can be tackled realistically and strategically. For example, an appraisal of priority tasks can be determined and energy can be devoted to accomplishing these as well as possible given the time constraints. On the other hand, this stressful situation can lead to a surge of energy which is used to procrastinate. The energy is not directed towards the challenge, but in avoiding the challenge. Unfortunately, the challenge does not go away: the tests and assignment are still on the student's plate. This is an example of the debilitating effect of negative stress. Rather than doing the best one can in the circumstance, the student is immobilized and the stressors continue to loom large.

An integral part of stress management is good time management. By employing good time management techniques, a student is more likely to benefit from positive stress rather than to be hindered by negative stress. Good time management allows the student to anticipate certain demands and to plan accordingly. In the event that particularly heavy demands are placed on the student, or unexpected demands surface, time management principles contribute to realistic, quality decision making. Good time management is one of the best tools that we have for managing stress.

▷ Individual Responses to Stress

There is an amazing range of human responses to the same kind of stressors. An observation during a long standstill in traffic demonstrates this. In one car, a man who was screaming into his car phone, veins bulging from his head, was obviously distressed. In another car, a woman, perhaps anticipating a traffic jam and coming prepared, was reading a book. In a third car, a young man appeared particularly relaxed. In the midst of the traffic congestion he was playing a flute! All three people were in the same situation, but all three were responding in different ways. While they could not control the situation -- there was nothing they could do to get the traffic moving -- they could control their responses to the situation.

Students share many of the same kind of stressors, and here too one can observe a variety of individual responses. Consider the following students.

It just didn't seem fair! *When the pressure was on, Leslie was at her best. In fact, she thrived during the days leading up to final exams. With her concentration skills at their peak, she could capture quality time and complete many planned study tasks effectively and efficiently. Unlike Leslie, Karyn crumpled under the stress of final exams. With the pressure on, she panicked, and when she wasn't spending study hours worrying, she was trying to cram each and every detail that she came across into her head. While Leslie entered her exams feeling confident and in control, Karyn was overwhelmed and distressed.*

Are you more like Leslie or Karyn? Leslie experiences positive stress that contributes to her motivation and concentration levels. Karyn's experience shows the debilitating effects of negative stress. If your academic performance is hindered by distress, it is time to take control and change your response to stressors.

RECOGNISING SYMPTOMS OF STRESS

Why should you spend time improving your stress management skills? Time management entails not only allotting a sufficient *quantity* of time to your studies, it also involves capturing *quality*. This is not possible when the stressors that are a part of academic life lead to negative stress. It is important to develop an awareness of how you respond to stressors in your life. There is likely a combination of physical, emotional, behavioural, and cognitive symptoms. By recognising personal symptoms of stress, you are better equipped to assess whether stress acts as a motivator or interferes with your academic effectiveness, and to intervene accordingly.

▷ Physical

Physical manifestations of stress are natural enough, but the symptoms that some people label as indicators of excitement that result in positive energy, others classify as evidence of a state of panic and distress. These symptoms may include an elevated heart rate, tightening of muscles, shallow breathing, and increased perspiration. Physical signs of distress may be demonstrated by increased susceptibility to illness, fainting, nausea and headaches.

▷ Emotional

Constant worrying, crying for no apparent reason, dependency on others or an extreme need to be alone, and lack of confidence may all suggest that stressors are contributing to negative stress, or distress, rather than positive stress. These emotional symptoms of stress can seriously erode quality time on coursework.

▷ Behavioural

Symptoms of negative stress may also be apparent in our behaviour. These may range from procrastination to acts of aggression, withdrawal, substance abuse, over or under sleeping, and to poor appetite or overeating. Extremes of many behaviours are often signals that we are experiencing distress.

▷ Cognitive

How we think and what we say to ourselves have a direct impact on stress levels. For example, some students think that if they cannot do an assignment perfectly, there is little point in doing it at all. Other students may convince themselves that it would be a 'catastrophe' if a certain mark is not attained; from a larger perspective, while it may be undesirable to get a lower mark than hoped for, it certainly is not devastating. These different types of thinking can lead to much distress.

What are your typical responses to stress?

Physical: _____

_____

_____

Emotional: _____

_____

_____

Behavioural: _____

_____

_____

Cognitive: _____

_____

_____

MANAGING DISTRESS

Academic stressors do not have to be the cause of distress. Rather, positive stress can act as a beneficial and motivating force on your studies. To restrict the debilitating effects of negative stress, consider incorporating the following techniques, along with good time management strategies, into your daily routine.

▷ Deep breathing exercises

If physical symptoms such as shallow breathing and a rapid heart beat are associated with distress, it is important to intervene so that these feelings do not increase in intensity. A quick way of capturing a feeling of calm is to take some slow, deep breaths. Concentrate on breathing in through your nose and out through your mouth, perhaps picturing yourself smelling a rose and then blowing out a candle. Do this about five or six times, and then resume normal breathing.

▷ Muscle relaxation

It is not uncommon for stress to be held in muscles; the shoulders, neck, and jaw are all particulary prone to tightening as stress builds. Sometimes, we are not even aware that stress is building until it has escalated to the point where our muscles are very tense and rigid. One way of ensuring that your stress level does not increase undetected is to engage in muscle relaxation techniques on a regular basis. These help to prevent distress by intervening before stress has a chance to build in the muscles undetected. Muscle relaxation techniques also serve to remind you what it feels like to be relaxed. Without this regular reminder, you may actually start to perceive the tense and rigid muscles as 'normal', making you particularly susceptible to the debilitating results of negative stress.

As the name implies, the main goal of this strategy is to relax the muscles. Muscle relaxation involves tightening your muscles, and then relaxing them. If you try to tighten a muscle and find that it is already tense, it is a sign that you are holding stress in that location, perhaps unknowingly. When engaging in muscle relaxation, you can target certain parts of your body that tend to become especially tense, or you can progress throughout your body from head to toe for an overall sense of calm. The contrast between the tense and relaxation states will help to increase your awareness of mounting stress levels and provide you with a sense of control over these responses. Muscle relaxation audiotapes are available to assist you. However, they are not necessary for you to benefit from this technique. What is required is a commitment to rehearse muscle relaxation on a regular basis.

▷ Exercise

The relationship between exercise and stress management can be discussed in reference to the 'fight-flight response'. Basically, what this suggests is when humans experience stress, especially if the stressor is perceived in any way as threatening, we are biologically equipped to 'fight' the stressor or 'flee'. The recognition of a threat results in a surge of energy to enable us to respond to the challenge. This mechanism works well when threatening stressors are wild animals or aggressive adversaries, but what happens when they are final exams or major seminars? This is where exercise enters the picture. As it is not desirable to physically fight or flee from these academic demands, exercise allows us to channel some of the building energy in a more constructive way. By providing us with a physical outlet for the surge of energy that comes with the identification of stressors, exercise helps to maintain stress at a manageable level.

It is important to keep in mind that exercise need not mean hours of rigorous workout. Relaxing walks, bicycling, or any of a variety of other activities are important stress management tools. By scheduling time to engage in a reasonable amount of exercise on a regular basis you are increasing the likelihood of capturing quality time for your academic pursuits.

▷ Self talk

It is said of people who talk to themselves that they do not have to worry until they start answering themselves too! But whether we realize it or not, we all talk *and* respond to ourselves. In fact, our stress level indicates a response to our self talk. If you are saying, *"This exam is going to be brutal! What if I fail! What about my future! I need to do well!"*, it is very likely that negative stress, in the form of worry and panic, will creep in and sabotage your effectiveness. On the other hand, you are likely to benefit from positive stress if you are saying, *"Yes this exam is going to be a challenge, and I really **want** to do well, so I'll do my best by making good use of the time that I can reasonably afford to spend on this course."* What you say to yourself directly affects your stress level.

Monitoring your self talk is not always an easy task. It is hard to control self talk if we are not aware of it. Start listening to yourself and ask, *"Would I say this to someone I care about?"* If the answer is *"no"*, work on 'thought stopping' and replacing your self talk with something less debilitating and more supportive. Be particularly careful about confusing wants with needs. Consider Natalie's situation.

> **Natalie is stumped.** *She cannot understand why she does so poorly on the Medical College Admission Test (MCAT). She works extremely hard to prepare for the test and she really wants to do well. In her conversation with a counsellor she says aloud what she has been saying to herself over and over again: "I need to be a doctor. My future happiness in life hinges on being a doctor."*

Is it any wonder that Natalie experiences distress during the MCAT? Through her self talk she has convinced herself that her entire future happiness as a human being depends on her performance on this one test. On examining her self talk Natalie acknowledged that while she really *wants* to pursue medical school, she does not *need* to accomplish this goal. By putting this goal in perspective, she was able to spend less time worrying and more time concentrating on the task at hand. As her self talk changed, negative stress became positive stress and her goal became more attainable.

 ▷ **Visual imagery**

Just as what we say to ourselves influences the type of stress that we experience, how we picture ourselves also has an impact. Consider the student who repeatedly thinks, *"I'm going to fail...I'm going to fail."* The student is rehearsing failing. While thinking these words, images of not knowing the answers to test questions, or having mental blanks while presenting a seminar, may be fuelling distress.

Visual imagery, however, can also be used to create positive stress. By replacing the distressful images with images in which you are in control and focused on the task at hand, you are rehearsing feeling positive about a challenging situation. One student used visual imagery to capture quality time in an exam by picturing herself in the classroom taking a slow, relaxing breath as she read each question. She reminded herself not to panic if the answer was not immediately apparent, and imagined herself maintaining her composure and thinking through the question by identifying important words that would help place it within the context of the course.

Another type of visual imagery can also help to manage stress. Relaxation imagery involves picturing a place where you feel relaxed and in control. Practice recreating this image in your mind so that you can easily retrieve it in a distressful situation and experience a calming sensation. A brief time spent on relaxation imagery may be sufficient to replace negative stress with positive stress and redirect your full concentration to the task at hand.

▷ **Sharing with others**

Sometimes it may seem particularly difficult to replace debilitating distress with motivating positive stress. Persistent worrying may interfere with concentration, or personal problems may continually absorb our time and energy. It is at times such as these that our greatest strength can be sharing our concerns with others. While family and friends may be an important support for you, keep in mind the resources that are likely available at your school. Many academic institutions have counselling services that provide students with a range of support people, including personal, learning skills, and career counsellors. By sharing your concerns with someone who has training as a helper and who can probably be more objective than family or friends, you can lighten the burden of carrying these thoughts and feelings inside. As well, strategies to handle these concerns *and* effectively manage your coursework can be discussed. If counselling services are not available at your school, you may want to consider seeking out a teacher who appears approachable and understanding.

A HEALTHY LIFESTYLE

The best way to ensure that stress works for you rather than against you is to incorporate a healthy lifestyle into your daily routine. In this way, your time management will reflect not only sufficient *quantity* of time on your studies, but a high level of *quality*. By capturing quality time, you will increase your efficiency and effectiveness as a student. A good beginning point is to maintain your stress busters throughout the academic year.

▷ **Maintaining stress busters**

Five exams in five days!!! What to do???

X *Pull all nighters, cut out all breaks and extracurricular activities, and live on fast food and caffeine*

✓ *Develop a realistic plan that makes good use of daytime hours, allows for breaks and sleep, and ensures adequate nutrition*

Good nutrition, general fitness, a social life, rest and relaxation...these are the ingredients of a healthy lifestyle. Unfortunately, sometimes when we most need these stress busters, they are overlooked; we feel that we do not have time to eat, take breaks, or sleep. Initially we may feel productive, but we are contributing to negative stress and are at risk of obstructing our effectiveness.

As a student, it is important to capture positive stress to maximize your concentration and memory skills. Consider the following examples of **what *not* to do** given the following components of a healthy lifestyle.

• nutrition

Marika has never lived away from home before and feels totally inadequate in the kitchen. Rather than learning a few recipes and supplementing her diet with fresh fruit and vegetables, she dines on macaroni and cheese, peanut butter sandwiches, and take-out pizza. On top of adjusting to life away from home, she's had a number of academic setbacks this year but blames them on her surprisingly poor health. With colds and flu and...pass the pretzels please... *Is there a connection here?*

• general fitness

Ian's marks have plummeted since coming to university, but he cannot understand why - he works so hard. In fact, he is so determined to do well at school that he's given up his true love: jogging. When in high school, he worked out regularly and his marks were in the 80s. Now, he doesn't take any time away from his studies to exercise and his marks are in the 50s! *Could it be that spending some time on his general fitness enhanced his studies by improving his motivation and concentration?*

• a social life

Tyler knows exactly what he wants out of the time management workshop in which he's enroled: to learn how to do all of his school work on Mondays and Tuesdays. That would leave the rest of the week for fun! Sebastian, on the other hand, doesn't want to allocate *any* time for socialising, after all, he is a serious student. Both students are struggling academically. They will learn in the workshop that *both* over-socialising and under-socialising may pose problems. *Does the answer lie somewhere in between with a schedule that allows for a reasonable amount of both social and academic activities?*

• rest and relaxation

Elaine absolutely loves residence life. There are always so many other people around that it is never dull and boring. The only drawback is lack of sleep. Enticed by all the activity going on around her, Elaine is finding it impossible to get any work done before midnight. This means working in the wee hours, missing early morning classes, and crashing for the better part of the weekend. Sure her marks are slipping and she's actually nodded off in a class, but doesn't this happen to everyone? *Perhaps there is something to the theory that sleep deprivation interferes with memory and concentration skills after all!*

Consider your own lifestyle. **Does your lifestyle enhance your effectiveness as a student by encouraging positive stress or does it sabotage your performance by fuelling distress?** By having a healthy lifestyle, you may be able to spend less time on your school work and achieve better grades than someone who loses quality time due to an unhealthy lifestyle. Use the following worksheet to help determine if there are actions that you can take to improve your academic effectiveness and efficiency.

Stress Buster	Questions to consider...	Actions for "no" responses...
Nutrition	Do you: • eat a healthy breakfast? • watch your caffeine intake? • have balanced nutritious meals? • include fresh fruits & vegetables in your diet? • feel satisfied with your present eating habits?	*e.g., Start planning for meals*
General Fitness	Do you: • exercise regularly? • walk or bike to nearby places? • usually feel in good health? • maintain exercise breaks even during busy, stressful times? • feel satisfied with your general level of fitness?	*e.g., Make time to walk to school.*
A Social Life	Do you: • balance academic demands with a social life? • *not* feel guilty for spending deserved breaks with friends? • feel satisfied that your social life enhances - *not* hinders - your academic pursuits?	*e.g., Use socialising as reward*
Rest & Relaxation	Do you: • get an adequate amount of sleep each night (i.e., 7 to 9 hours)? • incorporate breaks into your schedule to 'recharge'? • avoid worrying about school during scheduled breaks? • feel rested and energetic?	*e.g., No more all night cramming!*

QUESTIONS FOR REFLECTION

- *What is stress?*

- *What are the differences between positive and negative stress?*

- *How is good time management related to stress management?*

- *List your typical responses to stress, including examples of physical, emotional, behavioural and cognitive manifestations.*

- *What are some techniques for managing your negative stress?*

- *Specify the components of a healthy lifestyle that you incorporate into your daily routine.*

- *How could you improve your effectiveness and efficiency as a student?*

## Chapter 8

DEALING WITH CRISES

THE HUMAN CONDITION

THE EXPECTED

THE UNEXPECTED

QUESTIONS FOR REFLECTION

THE HUMAN CONDITION

Students are human. This statement may be obvious, but the implications for individual students are often overlooked. What this means is that as human beings students will experience setbacks. Even the best time managers procrastinate from time to time. Despite careful planning, many students feel overwhelmed at certain times. And there can be a fine line between too few and too many breaks, leaving room for errors in judgement. As human beings, difficult circumstances are bound to happen: one's health can deteriorate, a loved one can die, tension can surface in a valued relationship, or financial hardships can arise. These crises are normal happenings in the ups and downs of the human condition.

These crises are also your teachers. Through these experiences you learn about yourself and you change as you acquire wisdom and maturity. You may learn how to avoid a setback the next time, or discover that you have the strength to persist in spite of obstacles. You may realize that it is okay to ask for help. Your own experiences are not the only teachers; by tapping into help resources at your school you are benefitting from the experiences of others. In doing so, you can avoid some of the pitfalls of student life.

THE EXPECTED

▷ Problems with Exams and Assignments

A variety of crises can occur in relation to exams and assignments. While "crisis" might seem like a strong word, problems with an important exam or assignment can easily be perceived as a catastrophe by the individuals involved. Reflecting on first year in university, one student commented, *"I studied really hard and I didn't do very well at all. I think I'll remember that forever - I wasn't used to it; this was a new experience for me."* For some students the crisis is a turning point.

Everyone thought that Daniel would have a superb academic career. Throughout high school he never had a mark below 90% and he was the unanimous choice for valedictorian his graduating year. People were stunned to hear that he quit three months into his Engineering programme. Why? Vincent received marks that he had never seen before: a 70%, a 55%, a failure! This blow to his confidence was too much; he vowed that he would never return to school.

A blow to confidence does not have to lead to such drastic measures as quitting school. Rather, it can be a positive turning point. By assessing what went wrong, and identifying how to increase the likelihood of success the next time, the benefits of this learning experience can be realised. Inventor Thomas Edison summed this up with the comment, *"I failed my way to success."* It was only through setbacks that he could achieve his significant accomplishments.

An integral part of success on exams and assignments is time management. Preparation for exams and assignments needs to be coordinated with the daily maintenance tasks of attending classes, reading textbooks, doing problem sets, and reviewing lecture notes. It is not difficult to fall behind if you are unprepared for the rapid pace of the academic year. Too often falling behind contributes to harmful habits such as skipping classes and all-night cram sessions.

Think about the following suggestions, based on actual experiences of students, to increase the likelihood that crises will be few and far between.

"Get down to work early in the fall. I wish somebody had told me how much work there was. I've been trying extra hard all year trying to pull up the grades I got in October."

"I always try to do my reading for the upcoming class, even if I've fallen behind. This way at least I'm prepared for class and I'm not feeling as though I'm always playing catch up. If I can cover the information I missed before the exam, great. If not, I'll skim it for main ideas."

"I've learned to tap into help resources if writer's block sets in. I used to wait and hope that it would go away, but it would only get worse as the deadline approached. Now I find that by dropping by the writing centre or checking in with a counsellor I can set weekly goals, and if I have trouble, there's someone to help get me back on track."

The use of time management tools also can assist in minimising crises. Notice how the following student uses a schedule not only to organise and plan an approach to school, but to reduce anxiety.

> *"Each time I get an assignment due date or exam date I write it on my four month planner. That way I can see the whole term at a glance and prepare for particularly busy times well in advance. Every term there comes a time when I look at everything on my plate and think that there's no way that I can get everything done. But I've started saving these schedules, and when I start feeling overwhelmed, I pull out an old one as a reminder that I did - and I can - get everything done."*

And what happens if you are not able to get everything done? While it is certainly unadvisable to make a habit of it, you can speak to the course instructor regarding an extension. If there are extenuating circumstances, such as a serious illness, this is a reasonable request; once your health improves, it is unlikely that the need for such an accommodation would become a habit.

If there are no major extenuating circumstances that have contributed to your lack of success in completing the required tasks on time, you are well advised to work on your time management skills. Pay particular attention to Chapter 3, *"Time Management Principles,"* and Chapter 4, *"Your Action Plan"*. **While you may be familiar with the strategies presented, do you actually implement them?** If the answer is, *"no"*, make a conscious effort to do so. As well, if your time management effectiveness is sabotaged by procrastination or worrying, reread Chapter 6, *"Beating the Procrastination Habit,"* and Chapter 7, *"Experiencing Stress,"* and concentrate on reducing these debilitating habits.

Major exam periods can be particularly challenging times for students. While your best defense is a sound foundation - the result of attending classes and keeping up with readings and assignments - what happens when you have two exams on the same day or five exams in five days? Decisions about how time is allocated become especially important. Do you invest all your energy in the early exams at the expense of the latter ones? Obviously, this is not a good idea. Rather, study time needs to be allocated for all exams. As well, rest and relaxation cannot be overlooked. One way of increasing the likelihood that this will occur is to provide yourself with a "map", or a time planner, to guide you through the exam period. Consider the following full-time student's schedule. A full course load often requires a sizable time commitment during exam periods, but afterwards you can look forward to a well deserved break.

TIME PLANNER FOR THE EXAM PERIOD

✓ Allocate time for all courses - need less/more time on certain courses?
✓ Be realistic! Work within time constraints. Don't panic and think positively.

	Sun	Mon	Tues	Wed	Thurs	Fri	Sat
7:00- 8:00						<- BREAK	FAST ->
8:00- 9:00	<---------	- BREAK	FAST ------	-------------	----------->	*PREPARE*	*Do*
9:00-10:00	*STUDY*	*Review*	__HISTORY__	*work*	__FRENCH__	*FOR*	*Math*
10:00-11:00	*FOR*	*French*	__EXAM__	*on*	__EXAM__	*BUSINESS*	*Problem*
11:00-12:00	*HISTORY*	*Notes*	↓	*biology*	Swim	Swim	*Sets*
12:00- 1:00	<---------	------------	-- LUNCH	BREAK --	------------	------------	--------->
1:00- 2:00	*work*	*STUDY*	*Do*	__BIOLOGY__	*Do*	*PREPARE*	Relax
2:00- 3:00	*on*	*FOR*	*Math*	__EXAM__	*Math*	*FOR*	__MATH__
3:00- 4:00	*biology*	*HISTORY*	*Problems*	↓	*Problems*	*BUSINESS*	__EXAM__
4:00- 5:00	<---Take	a break -	go for a	walk, rest,	watch TV -	--------->	↓
5:00- 6:00	<---------	------------	--- S U P	P E R ---	------------	--------->	*Yahoo!*
6:00- 7:00	*Review*	*STUDY*	*work*	*Review*	*PREPARE*	__BUSINESS__	Dinner
7:00- 8:00	*French*	*FOR*	*on*	*French*	*FOR*	__EXAM__	Out &
8:00- 9:00	TV	*HISTORY*	*biology*	*Notes*	*BUSINESS*	|	a Movie
9:00-10:00	BREAK	Relax	Relax	Relax	Relax	↓	
10:00-11:00	<---------	Try to get	to bed by	11 so well	rested for	exams --->	

While this time planner for the exam period may appear heavy, on close inspection you will find that this student is planning on working eight or nine hour days during the exam period, a time commitment somewhat heavier than a full-time job. However, this schedule *still* leaves eight hours per day for sleep and another seven or eight hours per day for travel, errands, and breaks.

It is also important to be realistic. If family or work commitments need to be accommodated during the exam period, less time may be available for studying. In these situations it is especially important to have a solid knowledge base in individual courses prior to the exam period. Also, if you have many commitments and are in a program that has a very intensive exam period, such as the one on the previous page, decisions may have to be made about pursuing your goal on a part-time basis or reducing outside responsibilities during this important evaluation period.

While you may tackle your exam periods somewhat differently, this schedule demonstrates some effective time management strategies that you may want to incorporate into your own plan:

✓ *establish a daily routine (ie. getting up, eating & studying at similar times) to free up energy otherwise used in continually assessing what to do next*

✓ *plan time to eat, relax and exercise to ensure that these important stress-reducing activities are not overlooked*

✓ *be careful not to compromise sleep -- a tired brain is not very productive. Lack of sleep can interfere with memory and concentration skills; allow for some time to unwind before a reasonable bed time*

✓ *if possible, schedule some study times so that they correspond with exam times to provide practice working with the information in a similar state of mind*

✓ *reward yourself for a job well done to provide a positive association with exams and something to look forward to at the end of the exam period*

A final comment on time management problems with exams concerns the actual writing of exams. While it is not a good idea to be checking your watch every few minutes in an exam, some attention needs to be given to the time constraint. Be aware of how much each component of the exam is worth, and allot your time accordingly. Answering a question brilliantly is not worth it if this resulted in insufficient time for a second, equally weighted question; your maximum mark would only be 50%. Also, do not spend too much time on questions that pose difficulties for you. After a reasonable amount of time, move on to other questions. If time permits after the exam is completed, return to the troublesome questions.

▷ Presenting Seminars

One of the most commonly shared of human fears is speaking in front of a group. Thus, it is not surprising that presenting seminars can be dreaded by many students. While not all academic programmes require the presentation of seminars, for students who face this challenge a strategic approach can transform this experience from an uncomfortable predicament bordering on crisis to a manageable, and perhaps even enjoyable, exercise.

As with so many academic demands, time management is a crucial element of presenting seminars. Students need to plan both for the preparation of the seminar information and for the presentation of the seminar in class. Speaking in front of a group is all the more anxiety provoking when a person is feeling poorly prepared or overly prepared; too little or too much information for the allotted time can have a significant negative impact on the overall quality of the seminar. A well thought out plan can prevent seminars from being perceived as academic disasters. Think about the following suggestions for the (1) preparation and (2) presentation of seminars.

(1) **PREPARATION**	(2) **PRESENTATION**
• develop a plan: in the weeks leading up to a seminar schedule time for **researching the topic** *(library/ interviews)*, **organising materials, identifying themes** to be discussed, **establishing time guidelines** *(e.g., 5 minutes for introduction)*, **making visual aids** and **rehearsing**	• give a brief outline to provide a general overview *(e.g., I will begin by asserting that... Secondly, examples will be provided...and lastly, discussion questions will be circulated).*
• choose a topic that interests you - it is much easier to talk about something that you enjoy	• prominently highlight major themes on your notes, indicating how much time you plan to spend on that section *(e.g., Discussion - 10 min)*
• capitalise on personal experiences if possible *(e.g., travel, work, life experiences)* - these require less effort to remember and can enhance meaningfulness/audience attention	• include an introduction, body, and conclusion to provide a complete 'package'
• narrow focus to a manageable size - too broad a topic will overwhelm both you & your audience	• it's okay to be nervous - take a deep breath and look at a friendly face
• prepare mentally: emphasise the valuable learning experience; picture yourself in control in front of the class; you are the expert!	• follow your time guidelines fairly closely; don't lose track of time
	• you run the show: if a question brings the seminar off topic, actively redirect the focus; if questions are interfering with time constraints, ask that they be held until the end, time permitting

▷ **Social Overload**

> *Claire didn't know how she would tell her parents. As she read the words "insufficient grade points to continue", she felt a tightening of her chest and a lump in her throat. Oh, she knew she'd goofed off this year; in fact, she'd had a great time socially. She was so busy playing sports and meeting friends that school always seemed to get placed on the back burner. But in her wildest dreams she didn't think that she would fail out of school. She was wrong.*

Despite warnings, this scenario is reality for some students every year. There can be so many enticements to lure students away from books and assignments, including opportunities to participate in various activities from clubs to sports, as well as the chance to enjoy the company of other students. At times it can be hard to remember that the primary reason for being in school is to get an education. When social overload occurs, *"the best of times"* can easily become *"the worst of times."*

If you should experience a crisis, such as not receiving satisfactory grades, keep it in perspective. It is disappointing. People whom you care about may be hurt and angry initially. Your goals may take longer to attain. But you are human and you can recover from this setback. If you feel that you cannot recover from this blow, contact the counselling department at your school or seek professional assistance in the community in which you live.

What can you do to prevent social overload from hurting you academic performance? Good time management can ensure not only that adequate time is spent on school, but that time is also available for other interests and activities. When this has not been the case, the student has a few options. For example, if social overload has resulted in a one-year suspension from school, there are often appeal processes that can be employed to attempt to have the suspension waived. If this appeal is not successful, time away from school can be used as an opportunity for work experience and maturation. This break from school can be a time to clarify whether or not education is a priority, with the possible result that the student returns to school more motivated and focused than ever.

While social overload may not result in suspension from school, it can certainly lead to a lackluster academic record that can make a student uncompetitive for other academic programmes or employment. It is important to learn from mistakes and not let social overload block academic effectiveness year after year.

THE UNEXPECTED

Unlike the expected potential problems of student life, unexpected crises often catch students unaware and unprepared. These include illness, money problems, family problems and relationship difficulties. All can have a significant impact on time management.

If you should find yourself dealing with an unexpected crisis, it is important to keep a few things in mind. First, remind yourself that this setback is part of the ups and downs of the human condition. As such, there are many people, including instructors and counsellors, who will empathise with you; it is likely that they have experienced similar setbacks and can provide you with some sound advice. While you do not have to reveal the intimate details of your problem if you are uncomfortable doing so, talk with these people as soon as possible.

A second suggestion is to meet with a health professional, in the event of illness, or a counsellor for other crises. A record of the problem by professional support people is important if any appeals for extensions or exam rewrites become necessary. Lastly, be flexible. Life may not always unfold in the ways that you hoped, so a good approach is to adapt as best as possible. In the end you may find that the crisis made you stronger and wiser. A brief exploration of these problems reveals some possible approaches to dealing with the unexpected.

▷ Illness

It is not a good idea to write an exam if an illness is significantly interfering with concentration and energy levels. Time management is not just planning a sufficient *quantity* of time, it is also capturing *quality* of time. It is likely that both of these would be compromised in the event of illness. As soon as you are able, contact your instructor and request a postponement. As well, consult with a physician for medical documentation to support your request. Follow this same procedure if a lengthy illness should interfere with the completion of assignments.

▷ Money Problems

Careful budgeting is a way of life for many students. Try to plan carefully for the costs associated with school. If you should find yourself with money problems there are a few options. Most post-secondary schools have student awards and financial aid offices; you may qualify for a loan or a bursary. Part-time employment can also be sought, but this can have major implications for time management. If this option is pursued, be realistic and assess whether a reduced course load is advisable.

▷ **Family Problems**

It can be exceedingly difficult to capture quality time for school work if thoughts of family problems persist. Sometimes serious family matters demand one's attention. However, a question needs to be asked: **How best can you deal with family problems *and* attend to school responsibilities?** The answer may not be easy. If there is something that you can actually do, for example, take care of a sick loved one, the answer may be reducing school responsibilities or temporarily leaving school. If there is nothing that you can do except worry, the answer may be to seek supports to help you limit your worrying and function at a productive level. These supports can be informal, such as family or friends, or they can be formal, such as counsellors or spiritual leaders. As much as possible, you want to keep the stress associated with family problems from being exacerbated by problems with school.

▷ **Relationship Difficulties**

Conflict in, or the termination of, a valued relationship hurts. Resolving conflict or grieving for the loss are time consuming. Again the question arises: **How best can you cope with relationship difficulties *and* be an effective student?** Allotting time to deal with these feelings can help prevent them from overflowing into your every waking hour. This may include finding a friend who is a good listener, tapping into the counselling resources at your school, or keeping a journal to express in writing your thoughts and feelings. Try not to compound the problems of relationships with academic setbacks.

QUESTIONS FOR REFLECTION

- *List some expected crises that students can anticipate.*
- *How can you prevent certain problems with exams and assignments?*
- *What are some planning strategies for the exam period?*
- *Discuss seminar preparation and presentation techniques.*
- *What options exist if social overload undermines academic performance?*
- *How can you cope with unexpected crises?*
- *What question can you keep in mind when struggling with family problems or relationship difficulties?*
- *List steps that you can take in the event of illness or money problems.*

## Chapter 9

SPECIAL SITUATIONS

ALL STUDENTS ARE SPECIAL

TRANSITION ISSUES

> ▷ *Academic*
> ▷ *Social*

THE MATURE STUDENT

PART-TIME STUDIES

STUDENTS WITH DISABILITIES

LEARNING IN A SECOND LANGUAGE

THE GRADUATE STUDENT

APPRENTICESHIPS & PLACEMENTS
IN COOPERATIVE LEARNING PROGRAMMES

QUESTIONS FOR REFLECTION

ALL STUDENTS ARE SPECIAL

A student is a student is a student. If this were true, explanations and recommendations would be *'one size fits all'*. There would be no need to consider individual situations or to tailor information to suit specific needs. In reality, however, students come with a wide range of personalities, skills and situations. What works for one student may not work for another student. This reflects the fact that all students are special; they bring a unique perspective to the learning environment based on their personal life experiences and circumstances.

Despite individual differences, students sometimes share similar circumstances that warrant similar time management considerations. While appreciating individual differences within any group, an exploration of time management issues for a sample of identifiable groups provides some suggestions for students in these special situations.

TRANSITION ISSUES

The move to a different school, or even to a higher grade within the same school, can be difficult for some students. The progression from high school to post-secondary school, in particular, often poses special challenges to students. Issues related to the transition issues can pertain to both the academic and social aspects of a student's life, and may include adapting to living away from home for the first time, adjusting to large classes, coping with an emphasis on independent learning, and dealing with a heavy workload. All of these issues have important implications for time management.

▷ Academic

What have you been told about differences in learning at high school versus college or university?

_____

_____

_____

_____

_____

> *It was Sara's first exam since high school and she knew that she was in trouble. In high school Sara had been a 'natural' learner: she was always successful on tests without putting forth much effort. In fact, she never studied until the night before a test, and then she would only reread her notes a couple of times. On tests she found that she needed to repeat the information back in much the same way as she had memorized it. This test was different; she didn't just have to recall information, but apply it to demonstrate a sound understanding -- which, she realised too late, was lacking.*

There can be some significant differences between learning at high school and learning at college and university. In many post-secondary programmes students are expected to demonstrate an in-depth grasp of large volumes of information. Students are also expected to be independent learners: the bulk of learning occurs outside class, with lectures providing structure. While some students find this independence liberating, others struggle with the increased responsibility.

Regardless of how natural a learner someone was in high school, initial frustration with these learning differences is not uncommon if good time management skills are lacking. In commenting on this transition, one student said, *"It took me a while to get used to the work. Before this year I had never studied on a Friday night in my life - I didn't have to."* Devoting increased time to academic endeavours may feel like a sacrifice initially. With effective time management, however, this increased workload can become manageable and routine.

The challenge of learning in post-secondary programmes can be compounded by the learning environment: in some post-secondary institutions it is not uncommon to have first-year class sizes of more than 250 students. Unlike in high school where teachers tend to know their students by name, the anonymity of some first-year classes can make it easy for students to miss classes, arrive unprepared for lectures, or to pay little attention while in class.

An important time management strategy is to make good use of class time. Attending classes, being prepared for lectures, and noting the main ideas discussed, provide a sound knowledge base. When preparing for tests and exams the student with a strong foundation has the advantage of having the time necessary to review and apply the course materials. The student with a weak foundation is likely to be cramming to get through readings, struggling to make sense of other students' class notes, and feeling overwhelmed at the prospect of retaining all of the information.

▷ **Social**

> *"Look out world, here I come." These words race through Alek's mind as he takes in his new apartment. No one to tell him to get up, go to school, or do his homework. He's free, and he intends to enjoy every minute of it! He cranks up the music, and reaches for the phone. It's time to initiate his first 'home away from home' with the party of the century.*

For some students there are significant social developments associated with the transition from high school to post-secondary school. An example is living away from home for the first time, an experience that can bring feelings of exhilaration, incredible loneliness, or both! This adjustment period can play havoc with time management as inordinate amounts of time are spent enjoying the social side of school or feeling miserable and homesick.

Students who are revelling the most in their new-found freedom may least appreciate the responsibilities that come with it. One first-year student had an extremely busy social calendar: he was on a varsity sports team and the representative for his floor in residence, he organised card games at all hours of the night, and he never turned down the chance to venture downtown. As final exams approached he knew that he was totally unprepared. When asked how this could happen he responded, *"I didn't have my parents to keep me on track."*

At the post-secondary level it is assumed that students are adults who are accountable for the consequences of their actions. If they fall behind through socialising, the problem does not lie with the course, but with the choices made. When social activities are regularly chosen over academic responsibilities there is bound to be a negative impact on academic performance. The implementation of time management strategies can help to provide the best of both worlds - an enjoyable social life *and* a rewarding academic career.

For some students the major transition issue is not being caught up in social activities, but, rather, coping with homesickness and loneliness. An orientation week questionnaire at one school suggested that while outwardly students appeared to be focused entirely on fun, inwardly they were experiencing a mix of emotions: students wrote that they felt scared, overwhelmed and lonely. One student reported feeling disoriented during orientation week! These are normal feelings. It is likely that they will lessen as time passes and the new surroundings become familiar.

THE MATURE STUDENT

Returning to school as a mature student poses certain special challenges. The mature student often has many non-school responsibilities, such as family and a job. Time management becomes especially crucial when realistic schedules are necessary to accommodate a variety of priorities *and* still allow for rest and relaxation.

Along with these demands on time there is the adjustment to being a student again. While mature students often have many strengths, including a high degree of motivation and life experiences that can make course content more meaningful, confidence issues can emerge. One student recalled struggling through high school before quitting in despair. Out of school she started her own successful business, and years later, decided that it was time to fulfil her dream of attaining a university degree. She was capable and confident - until she walked through the door of a classroom. Then, all of her insecurities and anxieties from high school resurfaced.

It's been nineteen years since Ingrid last sat in a classroom, and she doesn't know if her heart is pounding so hard because she's excited or scared. Will she be able to compete with the other students? Most of them are fresh out of high school and young enough to be her children! It's been a long time since she's read textbooks, written essays, and studied for exams, and then it was a struggle. What if she can't keep up with the course? Where will she start? She wonders if returning to school was a good idea.

Negative past associations with school can interfere with time management. While a sufficient *quantity* of time may be available, the *quality* of time may be diminished by worry and stress. To build confidence it can be a good idea to ease into being a student again; rather than starting with a full course load, consider taking a course or two in subject areas that you find particularly interesting. As well, *before* starting a programme, determine if upgrading in a particular area, for example math, is advisable. Time and energy can be lost if the necessary background is lacking.

Whether past recollections of school are positive or negative, locate resources that facilitate re-entering school. For example, you may find mature student advisors who provide direction with course requirements and learning skills and career counselling services that offer support programmes. Find out if there is a "Mature Student Association" that offers the chance to learn from the experiences of peers.

PART-TIME STUDIES

> *John feels as though he has it all. He loves the variety of his week: a class on Monday evening, a job with flexible hours, mornings with his infant daughter, and time to spend honing his carpentry skills. Sure his friends tease him that his baby will graduate before he does, but he likes the pace. He has the energy and enthusiasm to put forth a good effort most of the time.*

Pursuing an education on a part-time basis can be a wise decision. The reasons for deciding to be a part-time student may include family or work responsibilities, health issues, to ease into school after an absence, or to take a break from full-time studies to get some distance to determine academic or career goals.

The decision to opt for part-time studies can reflect an appreciation of what it takes to be a good time manager. A realistic appraisal of individual circumstances helps to assess the number of activities that can be juggled at a given time. There may be a limitless number of things that you would do *if* you were not bound by the number of hours in a week. With a limit of 168 hours, however, decisions have to be made regarding how best to allocate time. If there are many demands on time, part-time studies may be the perfect solution: you have the opportunity to get an education and still attend to day-to-day matters without becoming overwhelmed.

Regardless of the underlying motivation for enroling in part-time studies, effective time management is necessary to ensuring that sufficient quality time is allocated for course work. This may be particularly challenging for the part-time student who has other major commitments. One part-time student struggled with academic deadlines because she did not want to let others down. Her boss, her partner, her children, and even her dog, received her attention before her school work. After all, she reasoned, they all depended on her.

While academic pursuits may not be the only responsibility that a person has, they still need to be considered a priority. To improve time management the part-time student may need to say, *"no"*, to others more often and not feel guilty for dedicating time and energy to personal and academic goals.

Establishing contact with instructors, counsellors, and other students may be especially valuable for part-time students. These relationships can increase a sense of belonging to the academic community, which in turn can contribute to overall effectiveness.

STUDENTS WITH DISABILITIES

There are a wide range of disabilities represented within the student population. Students with hearing or visual impairments, learning disabilities, physical disabilities, and chronic illness are an integral part of the student community. While many academic and social issues are the same for all students, there are some circumstances in which students with disabilities may find themselves that have a special impact on time management.

Consider the student who uses a wheelchair or scooter. While many schools claim to be fully accessible, this may not quite be the case. A preponderance of stairs, curb cuts that are few and far between, and unreliable or inconveniently located elevators (for example, in a loading dock!) provide the student with a mobility impairment with a 'unique' perspective.

The hassle of taking long detours to get to classes or the discouragement of dropping a course because of its inaccessible location are unfortunate realities for some students. Until schools become truly accessible, a student who uses a wheelchair or scooter is least likely to miss all or part of a class if that student has a schedule in place that allows extra time in between classes.

Many schools have a person designated to coordinate services for students with disabilities. This person can inform students with mobility impairments of campus accessibility, including the location of elevators and ramps. Realistic course schedules may also be arranged with the help of this person's expertise. As well, information on other important services is available. Some campuses have access vans that provide campus transportation for people with mobility impairments. This can be a valuable time saver, especially in bad weather conditions.

An important time management strategy for all students with disabilities is to locate available services. Assistive devices, such as tape recorders and spell checkers, may be available for loan to improve effectiveness and efficiency. Some schools have computer facilities for students with disabilities, and resource people who can inform students about getting books on audiotapes or arranging for notetakers. The objective of these services is to lessen disadvantages that a student may experience relative to his or her peers because of a disability.

Special attention to specific time management principles may be particularly crucial for students with certain disabilities. For example, students with attention deficits or chronic pain may especially benefit from finding and using a good work location, using "best times" for school work, and subdividing large tasks into manageable smaller tasks. All students are wise to locate useful resources and develop a time management action plan, but these strategies may be especially crucial for the academic success of students with specific disabilities.

LEARNING IN A SECOND LANGUAGE

The challenge of working with abstract concepts and specialised terminology written in a language other than your first language is substantial. Despite this demanding situation, there are no more hours in the week and the term progresses as rapidly as ever. Students in this situation *need* to be strategic. Consider the following time-saving strategies:

✓ *before reading, look over the chapter. Pay special attention to headings and subheadings, words in bold text or italics, and summaries. This strategy can make the actual reading more meaningful and increase reading rates.*

✓ *always attend class unless there is a very good reason for missing it. While in class try to learn as much as possible - what are the main ideas? List new words in the margin of your notebook. Listen for clues, such as, "This would make a good exam question" and mark them in your notes.*

✓ *review class notes within 24 hours of taking them. If you do not understand them, talk to the instructor or a classmate. Think about the information and ways of remembering the main ideas and any new words.*

While it may be tempting, try not to sacrifice sleep. Initially it may seem as though more work is accomplished, but chronic sleep deprivation increases the risk of illness and may interfere with memory skills. It is a challenge to learn in a second language. Language skills can be enhanced by practising the second language daily. Read newspapers or magazines for relaxation and talk with instructors and peers.

THE GRADUATE STUDENT

> *Selina is starting to think that she will never finish her thesis. She can no longer remember what it feels like to be truly excited about her research; she just wants to get it done and carry on with her life. She's tired of being broke, and she dreads the feelings of guilt that overtake her when she takes a break from her work.*

The completion of a graduate thesis is in some ways the ultimate test of a person's time management skills. This major independent research project can absorb years of a person's life and be plagued with setbacks. Initially, course work may provide a diversion from this obligation, but eventually, the abbreviation for "all but dissertation" can become a nagging reminder that the student is "all but done".

A number of time management strategies that can make this project manageable have been discussed in this book. **Indicate if you use the following strategies. If you do not, plan on trying them in the upcoming week.**

✓	X	TIME MANAGEMENT STRATEGIES
		• *set goals* - establish goals and set tentative deadlines (e.g., focus on literature review this month; conduct data analysis over summer months)
		• *flag start dates* - use a calendar to target start dates for different components of the thesis. Be realistic & flexible
		• *subdivide large tasks into smaller, manageable tasks* - (e.g., write a paragraph summarising an article versus "I'll write the literature review")
		• *write "to do" lists* - identify tasks to be accomplished in the upcoming week; prioritise in order of importance (e.g., *contact Pat re: funding)
		• *make daily plans* - see "to do" list for reasonable daily goals. Plan for relaxation to 'recharge' - overwork can decrease productivity/motivation
		• *find a good work location* - do work that requires concentration away from high traffic locations or distractions (e.g., talkative office mates)
		• *use "best times"* - consider when you get your best work done & reserve these times for thesis work. A routine can save time deciding what to do
		• *establish limits* - don't be afraid to say *"no"*. (e.g., one helpful-to-a-fault student finally told colleagues not to interrupt until his thesis was complete)
		• *regular check-ins* - schedule regular meetings with advisors to discuss progress. Keep on track by meeting with a supportive friend or counsellor

APPRENTICESHIPS & PLACEMENTS
IN COOPERATIVE LEARNING PROGRAMMES

There are some programmes that provide students with both academic credentials and work experience. Nursing, early childhood education, and library and information science are just three examples of such programmes. Students in these programmes are in the special situation of having to adjust to two systems during the course of their studies.

Sometimes this shift in experience occurs within the same week. In other programmes, the student experiences school and practicums in alternating blocks of weeks or months. Regardless of the specific situation, adjustments to individual approaches to time management are likely. Time has to be planned for academic tasks, as well as for any preparation or follow-up associated with the work experience component of the programme. Also, special consideration may have to be given to any additional travel time that arises.

Many of the basic time management principles that have been discussed throughout this book are particularly relevant for students in apprenticeships and with placements in cooperative learning programmes. For example, planning ahead and recording important events is an important strategy for all students, but perhaps even more so for a student who is undergoing the alternating demands of school and work experience. If you are in this special situation, make sure that you are familiar with the time management strategies that are presented in this book, and that you are actively implementing those that best suit your particular circumstances.

QUESTIONS FOR REFLECTION

- *Describe some transition issues that are related to learning.*

- *What are some effective time management strategies to deal with a new learning environment?*

- *What advice would you give a student entering college or university regarding the social aspect of student life?*

- *How can negative past associations with school interfere with time management?*

- *Discuss the advantages and disadvantages of attending school on a part-time basis.*

- *What are some possible resources for students with disabilities?*

- *Discuss the importance of time management for students who are learning in a second language, graduate students, or in placement programmes.*

Chapter 10

AND WHAT ABOUT THE FUTURE?

CULTURAL MESSAGES ABOUT TIME

> ▷ **A Social Construct**

A student who is a "New Canadian" was talking one day about the wonders of Canada. *"You know"*, he said, *"Canada is such a rich country. It has education, housing, lots of food in the stores and goods to buy. But the one thing that Canada is very short of is -- TIME. Everyone here is in such a hurry. No-one has much time to talk. They're always rushing off somewhere because they have so much to do. In my country the days were really long and slow. They seemed to go on for ever."* Does this observation make you stop and think?

Canada is very typical of modern industrialised countries of the world. In its main population centres, the pace is fast and time is of the essence. How many people do you know who do not wear a wristwatch? It is probably a very small number. Getting one's first watch is almost what an anthropologist calls a "rite of passage". This is one of those events that indicate that we belong to a particular group. Learning to tell the time is such an important goal of our society that children are often given toy clocks and watches to facilitate early development of the concept of time through play. Even the name "*watch*" is a clear indication of what we expect to do with time!

Cultures differ in their beliefs and values about time. On a TV programme about dance in religious ceremonies, a Nigerian was explaining the beautiful, gentle movements associated with dances of the old religion in Nigeria. The movements were very rhythmic and unhurried. He said, *"These movements parallel life. They represent patience. In our dealings with people in Nigeria, patience is a very important quality."* There are many other cultures, like that of Nigeria, in which the concept of time is slower than ours: where patience is practised and expected. Cultures have evolved over centuries and the concept of time has been constructed differently by the various societies. The Spanish word "*siesta*," for example, does not have an English equivalent and yet we all know what it means. The term "*afternoon nap*" hardly captures the meaning of the traditional respite from the heat of the day. We may not have the word "siesta" in our language, but how many people in North America experience that slowing down in the early afternoon, especially in the hot weather, as they try to maintain high productivity?

Cultures teach values, including values about time. For you to understand fully your own experience with time, it is important for you to put it into the context of the society in which you live. What has your society taught you about time management?

▷ **The Society in which we Live**

Society sends clear messages about the role that time plays in people's lives. On some TV channels, time is on constant display and viewers can set their watches to within a micro-second. We live in a culture in which time matters and success is often measured by speed. For many people the few weeks of the year when they are on holiday and can enjoy the slower pace of unhurried living are a welcome change from the fast pace of work and school. Others even prefer to vacation at a fast pace and get bored quickly if there is a lull in activities. Whether we choose to fit with society's expectations about time, choose to ignore them, or fight against them, society has influenced the way in which we all view and manage time.

FAST IS BETTER:

A pervasive message from our own society is that "fast is better." With transportation, such as cars, trains, planes, bikes, skis and even roller blades, one of the major selling points is speed. How quickly can they get us from point A to point B? We expect tools to do the job as quickly as possible; office computers are getting faster all the time; touch telephones are rapidly making the telephone dial obsolete; the check-out counter at the supermarket uses computer scans to total the grocery bill; the instabank machine has replaced the line up at the bank. Fast is in and those who do not move or think fast can be left behind in our modern society.

TIME IS LIMITED:

We are also bombarded with the idea that "time is limited." How often do you see signs that proclaim, *"for a limited time only"*, *"weekly specials"*, or *"time is running out"*. We get the message that we had better make up our minds quickly, otherwise we will miss the boat! As students, we live with the time limits of tests and exams. The academic testing situation evaluates far more than knowledge of the course content; it also tests our ability to work within time limits.

TIME IS MONEY:

The business concept of "time is money" directs us to save time because, when we waste time, we are wasting something of measurable value. Office desks are located with accessibility in mind. You may have set up your own workspace at home based on the same principle. Also, it costs a lot of money to be a student, and so students will often plan to graduate as quickly as possible for budget reasons. Saving time is always a most persuasive argument, for example, to rationalise driving the car to school instead of walking, cycling, or taking public transportation.

▷ **Early Messages**

Children learn messages about time that may direct the way they manage time as adults. Consider the recollections of the following individuals. **As you read through their experiences, check to see if you received the same social messages.**

Terry "I always remember being told to think before I did something. **THINK FIRST** was the big message. I find that now that I'm working, and having to juggle twenty different things on a single day, I use that principle all the time. If I plan my activities before I get started, then everything seems to get done much faster."

David "I was always involved in a lot of different things, even by grade four. My parents didn't like us to watch too much TV. If I was off playing hockey for hours on end, that was O.K. I was expected to **GET INVOLVED IN MEANINGFUL ACTIVITIES** and to learn something from them. I am still very involved, especially with swimming and music and I love to read."

Susan "I was always the dawdler in our house, especially in the mornings. I used to drive my older sister crazy. We went to school together and she was always telling me to **HURRY UP**. Now her son is just like I was as a child and she is going through it all over again! I think that I am now a really good time manager. However, I still look forward one day to living in the country where the pace is much slower."

Jim "It was drilled into us that we should **ALWAYS BE ON TIME**. This came mainly from my father. He thought that it was so impolite to be late and that it reflected negatively on one's character. If we were going somewhere, he would pace up and down waiting for the rest of the family. It was a big family joke and we used to tease him about it, but now I find that I do just the same thing myself!"

Your own experience?

_____

_____

_____

_____

TIME MANAGEMENT IN THE WORKPLACE

▷ **On the Job**

If you can develop good time management skills as a student, you will find that these skills are highly valued in the workplace. It is very difficult, without a crystal ball, to say what the work world of the future will look like. However, it is likely that people will need to be self motivated and flexible about many aspects of work. Work situations are likely to be different. For example, you might be linked, via a computer network, to people in different parts of the country, or even the world. This is already happening, as computer and telecommunications technologies constantly develop. Workers of the future will need to have high-level time management skills and, when seeking employment, be able to list and describe these skills clearly.

This book has described many strategies that deal with all aspects of time management. Keep these in mind as you imagine that you have to write a resumé emphasising your time management ability and skills.

List six skills that will enable you to be very efficient on the job. For each, describe clearly and briefly the experiences that allowed you to develop this skill.

SKILL	EXPERIENCES

LIFELONG LEARNING

The educational world of the future is just as likely to look very different as is the world of work. Many more people will be involved in a continuing, lifelong educational process. This is already happening. The fastest growing sector of the post-secondary educational market is that of the mature student. As jobs demand higher and higher levels of education, adults are returning to schools, colleges and universities in large numbers. Many of these students have found that they need to develop new knowledge and marketable skills to compete in the job market.

There is also a strong trend for workers on-the-job to upgrade skills through courses offered to meet the needs of specific occupations. In addition, with changing demographics, the number of retirees is growing. This population too is getting more involved in formal education as a way of enriching the post-retirement years.

Adults often require flexibility in the way in which they access services, because of more involvement in family and work commitments. Therefore, adult students are, more and more, taking courses through correspondence, teleconferencing, television, and at on-the-job locations. Changes such as these are likely to continue and to develop in new directions in the future. It seems clear that the worlds of education and of work will be less separate in the future than they have been in the past. People will be more likely to continue their formal education throughout their life span.

In the future, managing time as a student will mean different things to different people, and will depend largely on how many other essential activities they have to coordinate with course work. A clear grasp and effective application of positive time management principles will ensure that lifelong learning is a quality experience.

GOAL CHECK

Throughout this book you have been invited to make decisions about your own time management system. This interactive approach aimed to optimise application of the ideas to your specific time management needs. In Chapter One, *"You and Time,"* you assessed your approach to time management and selected five items from the assessment inventory that you felt were in need of improvement at that time. These five items were your initial goals. Look back at those goals now to evaluate your progress. **What has been your progress in improving on those five items?**

_____

_____

_____

_____

_____

FINDING THE RIGHT BALANCE

This book has been about managing time as a student. It has made the important assumption that managing time effectively is a personal goal for you. It has explored aspects of what time means to you, as well as to typical students with whom you may be in contact. It has offered positive time management principles and encouraged personal interpretation and application of the ideas.

This book has recognised that effective time planning is more than simply writing down the tasks you have to do. Understanding what motivates you to do work as a student, and having effective strategies at hand to manage procrastination, general stress and occasional crises, are integral parts of an effective time management system. This book has put the concept of time into a cultural context and explored how each one of us learns about time from those around us and from society at large.

Only you can determine the right balance between school work and all of the other demands on your time. If you can get a handle on a good system for you, you will accomplish much and feel good about the experience. Once you have chosen positive time management principles and have applied them regularly, good time management habits will follow. It is up to you to make your time management system work well for you.

SUMMARY REFLECTIONS

_____

_____

_____

_____

_____

_____

_____

_____

_____

_____

_____

_____

_____

_____

_____

_____

_____

_____

_____

APPENDIX A

THE ASSESSMENT INVENTORY

Use the table below to compare your score to a representative sample of other students. The table gives percentile rankings. For example, if your score on the assessment inventory was "7", your percentile ranking is "66.0". That means that your score was higher than the scores of 66 per cent of the representative sample of students who completed the questionnaire. Data for the table were collected from 200 students from a variety of classes and educational institutions.

score	percentile	score	percentile	score	percentile
31	100.0	9	73.9	-7	21.3
26	99.5	8	70.7	-8	20.7
24	98.9	7	66.0	-9	19.1
22	98.4	6	63.3	-10	17.0
21	96.8	5	60.1	-11	12.8
20	96.3	4	55.9	-12	10.1
19	95.7	3	52.1	-13	8.5
18	93.1	2	47.3	-14	7.4
17	92.0	1	42.6	-15	5.3
16	89.4	0	38.3	-16	4.3
15	85.6	-1	36.2	-17	3.2
14	85.1	-2	34.0	-20	2.7
13	83.5	-3	30.9	-22	2.1
12	81.4	-4	28.7	-23	1.6
11	79.3	-5	25.0	-25	1.1
10	76.6	-6	23.9	-37	0.5

Your score_____   Your Percentile Ranking_____

APPENDIX B

ORGANIZERS

Tear out the blank organizers in Appendix B and use them to help you to organise your study time. Use these organizers as masters, that is, make photocopies and keep the blank copies from this book to use again. If you need more space on the organizers, you may wish to enlarge them on a photocopier. For specific guidelines regarding the use of these organizers refer to Chapter 4, *"Your Action Plan."*

WEEKLY SCHEDULE

	Mon	Tues	Wed	Thur	Fri	Sat	Sun
7:00- 8:00							
8:00- 9:00							
9:00-10:00							
10:00-11:00							
11:00-12:00							
12:00- 1:00							
1:00- 2:00							
2:00- 3:00							
3:00- 4:00							
4:00- 5:00							
5:00- 6:00							
6:00- 7:00							
7:00- 8:00							
8:00- 9:00							
9:00-10:00							
10:00-11:00							

WEEKLY SCHEDULE

	Mon	Tues	Wed	Thur	Fri	Sat	Sun
7:00- 8:00							
8:00- 9:00							
9:00-10:00							
10:00-11:00							
11:00-12:00							
12:00- 1:00							
1:00- 2:00							
2:00- 3:00							
3:00- 4:00							
4:00- 5:00							
5:00- 6:00							
6:00- 7:00							
7:00- 8:00							
8:00- 9:00							
9:00-10:00							
10:00-11:00							

Sun	Mon	Tues	Wed	Thur	Fri	Sat

Sun	Mon	Tues	Wed	Thur	Fri	Sat

Sun	Mon	Tues	Wed	Thur	Fri	Sat

Sun	Mon	Tues	Wed	Thur	Fri	Sat

"TO DO" LIST FOR WEEK OF _____

#	COURSE WORK TASKS	✓
1		
2		
3		
4		
5		
6		
7		
8		
9		
10		
12		

	PERSONAL	✓
1		
2		
3		
4		

UPCOMING MAJOR TESTS AND ASSIGNMENTS		DATE
1		
2		
3		

"TO DO" LIST FOR WEEK OF _____

#	COURSE WORK TASKS	✓
1		
2		
3		
4		
5		
6		
7		
8		
9		
10		
12		

	PERSONAL	✓
1		
2		
3		
4		

UPCOMING MAJOR TESTS AND ASSIGNMENTS	DATE
1	
2	
3	

DAILY PLANS

For_____

#	STUDY TASK	LOCATION AND TIME	✓
1			
2			
3			
4			

For_____

#	STUDY TASK	LOCATION AND TIME	✓
1			
2			
3			
4			

For_____

#	STUDY TASK	LOCATION AND TIME	✓
1			
2			
3			
4			

DAILY PLANS

For_____

#	STUDY TASK	LOCATION AND TIME	✓
1			
2			
3			
4			

For_____

#	STUDY TASK	LOCATION AND TIME	✓
1			
2			
3			
4			

For_____

#	STUDY TASK	LOCATION AND TIME	✓
1			
2			
3			
4			

READER REPLY CARD

We are interested in your reaction to *Power over Time: Student Success with Time Management.* You can help us to improve this book in future editions by completing this questionnaire.

1. What was your reason for using this book?
   - ☐ university course
   - ☐ college course
   - ☐ continuing education course
   - ☐ professional
   - ☐ personal development
   - ☐ other interest _____
   _____

2. If you are a student, please identify your school and the course in which you used this book.

3. Which chapters or parts of this book did you use? Which did you omit?

4. What did you like best about this book? What did you like least?

5. Please identify any topics you think should be added to future editions.

6. Please add any comments or suggestions.

7. May we contact you for further information?

   Name: _____

   _____

   Address: _____

   _____

   _____

   Phone: _____

(fold here and tape shut)

0116870399-M8Z4X6-BR01

Heather McWhinney
Publisher, College Division
HARCOURT BRACE & COMPANY, CANADA
55 HORNER AVENUE
TORONTO, ONTARIO
M8Z 9Z9

DATE DUE